Kevin
McCloud's
LIGHTING
BOOK

Kevin
McCloud's
LIGHTING
BOOK

THE ULTIMATE GUIDE
TO LIGHTING EVERY ROOM
IN THE HOME

SPECIAL PHOTOGRAPHY
BY MICHAEL CROCKETT

EBURY PRESS

London

For Grace

ABBREVIATIONS USED IN THIS BOOK

BC Bayonet cap.

ES Edison screw. The Edison screw and bayonet (see BC) designs for light bulbs have now become universal. The sizes available vary from country to country, however, according to the design of the fitting. (See also SBC, SES.)

GLS General Lighting Services. This is the classic incandescent ordinary tungsten bulb whose shape has hardly changed from Thomas Edison's original version.

ISL Internal-silvered lamp.

LES Lilliput Edison screw. Smaller sizes of the Edison screw fittings.

MES Miniature Edison screw. (See LES.)

PAR Parabolic aluminized reflector.

SBC Small bayonet cap. Most chandeliers are fitted with these.

SES Small Edison screw. Most chandeliers are fitted with these.

First published in 1995

1 3 5 7 9 10 8 6 4 2

Text copyright © Kevin McCloud 1995   Special photography copyright © Michael Crockett 1995
Illustrations copyright © Ebury Press 1995

Kevin McCloud has asserted his right under the Copyright, Designs and Patent Act, 1988 to be identified as the author of this work.

First published in the United Kingdom in 1995 by Ebury Press, Random House, 20 Vauxhall Bridge Road, London SW1V 2SA

Random House Australia (Pty) Limited, 20 Alfred Street, Milsons Point, Sydney, New South Wales 2061, Australia

Random House New Zealand Limited, 18 Poland Road, Glenfield, Auckland, New Zealand

Random House South Africa (Pty) Limited, PO Box 337, Bergvlei, South Africa

Random House UK Limited Reg. 954009

A CIP catalogue record for this book is available from the British Library.

ISBN 0 09 178383 6

Edited by Joanna Copestick and Emma Callery   Designed by Paul Welti   Typeset by Peter Howard
Picture research by Nadine Bazar   Illustrations by The R & B Partnership

Colour separations by Magnacraft, London   Printed and bound in Italy by New Interlitho Italia S.p.a., Milan

All instructions, information and advice given in this book are believed to be true and accurate at the time of going to press, and neither the author nor publishers can accept responsibility for any changes which may have occurred since. All guidelines and warnings should be read carefully and the author and publisher cannot accept responsibility for injuries or damage arising out of a failure to comply with the same.

CONTENTS

FOREWORD

*All material in nature, the mountains and the streams
and the air and we, are made of Light which has been spent,
and this crumpled mass called material casts a shadow, and
the shadow belongs to light.*

LOUIS KAHN (1901-1974)

I wrote this book because I wanted to know how to
light my own home properly. I had long since sus-
pected that low-voltage downlighters were not the
universal panacea to lighting problems. Indeed, like
most shop lighting that works its way into the
domestic market, I've often thought their glare and
sharp shadows highly inappropriate to most domestic situations.

Instead, I developed a simple system that is based
on five types of lighting that can be used separately
or in combinations, according to the rooms they are
used in. Once you have become acquainted with
them (see pages 8-13) you can begin to analyze any
lighting scheme – and begin to design your own.

Lighting designers recognize at least four of
these types, so I am trumpeting nothing new there.
But what is perhaps original is the way in which I
have mercilessly applied these five types to virtually
every photograph in this book, analyzing each
image. In addition, the initial sections to each chapter cover one location which we lit in three different
ways and then analyzed to show the relevant levels
of the five different types of light. Towards the end
of the book and designed to further help you plan
your lighting scheme, you will also find a large section dedicated to bulbs (known as sources) and
light fittings (known as luminaires) – the
Photographic Glossary (see pages 108-34).

Any lighting designer will start with the space he
or she is to light. And above all else, the designer
will look at what space is FOR. This is a key element. You may think that lighting design is about
the seductive lighting of your interior, since good
decoration (or even bad decoration) can be transformed into something miraculous with good light-

ing. But homes are not static showpieces, we have to live in them, and any good lighting design will first take into account what we do in the different rooms of our homes. Every activity, whether it is eating, relaxing, working, or making love, needs a different lighting 'state' that gives on the one hand the right level of light to see what we are doing, and on the other, the appropriate mood. So this book's chapters each tackle one room in the house and lists the two or three essential lighting elements needed there.

Arm yourself with this book, and use it as it is intended: as a hard-working tool to help you improve your lighting, flatter your decoration and make your home a more pleasant place to be.

KEVIN McCLOUD

INTRODUCTION

Five Types of Lighting

The way we like to light our interiors revolves around what we need the light for, since our tasks and activities range from cooking and cleaning to watching television and being intimate. In order to do our decorative schemes justice, we need not only different levels of brightness, but also different moods and emotional qualities in our lighting.

To help us understand lighting and to build up good schemes, it is useful to know that there are five basic types of lighting. Each one is characterized by their own mood and pragmatic value and we have created the five types here using ordinary kitchen implements to show how each one looks. Indeed they are so important, that every case study

photographed in this book has been analyzed in terms of these five types.

1 Ambient Lighting

As the name suggests, ambient light is that which is all around us. It is the light of a grey sky, where the clouds act as a giant lampshade in diffusing the sun's rays. It is light that is not from an obvious small source and one which creates hardly any shadow.

Indoors, the most obvious example of ambient light is that given off by a fluorescent strip or light housed in an opaque uplighter, which hides the light source. It lights the ceiling, which acts rather like grey clouds, playing the role of a giant reflector – it is as though it were made of glass and lit from behind.

Wallwashers are also good sources of ambient lighting: they illuminate a wall so it too can play the role of a reflector. The effect is extremely calming and neutral, since there is no glare to distract the eye.

(ABOVE) *With ambient light the source is hidden and the light cast over a wide area.*

(RIGHT) *A PAR lamp has its own silvered back, giving off ambient light with little glare, making it a powerful uplighter.*

In any room, ambient light gives us an ideal background light upon which we can build a room's character, using the other four types of light. But the essential rooms to install it in are the living room, kitchen and study. It is the perfect background light for watching television, and is also the obvious choice for giving a practical level of lighting in historic houses as a background to say, candle lighting, where the sources can be hidden on top of cupboards and in cornices and architraves; sited here and dimmed, their presence and their effect go unrecognized.

Ambient light sources should always be dimmable (making fluorescents out of the question) and as discreet as possible, although a feature can be made of a pendant bowl (see page 83) or of a wallwasher (see page 42). Even an enormous lampshade can give us an attractive and effective ambient light source.

(BELOW) *The large paper shades and screens in this room filter both daylight and artificial light. They combine both ambient and decorative lighting effects.*

2 Accent Lighting

Within a general ambient lighting scheme, accent lighting will enable you to add interest, highlighting features such as pictures, objects and architectural elements. By definition, accent lighting is restricted to a single area and can take the form of directional spotlighting, a table lamp with an opaque shade, or even a tungsten striplight mounted inside an unused fireplace.

Ambient lighting usually flattens a room, but accent lighting brings back the character and interest. Low-voltage halogen lighting is particularly suited to providing accent lighting on three counts. It gives a white light that contrasts well in an overall warm ambient setting of tungsten lighting; it has a small and bright light source that casts crisp shadows – particularly useful for lighting objects; and most fittings come with an integral reflector (flood, spot and mini-spot are available), which

allows for precise control over which areas are lit.

Low-voltage systems can often be mounted within the ceiling, or you can buy simple plug-in moveable lamps for uplighting a feature or grazing a wall with a patch of light, to bring out its texture.

Rooms that particularly benefit from accent lighting are the dining and living rooms, where the decorative value of the room's architecture, its colouring and displayed objects can be most

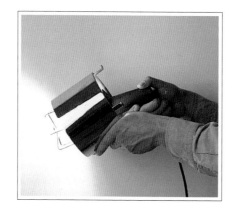

admired. But if you have a strong architectural feature in any room, even the toilet, highlight it.

(TOP) *This room is lit entirely with accent lighting, most of it from the stalk-like arrangement of low-voltage halogen spotlights.*

(ABOVE) *A small reflector bulb is ideal for accent lighting since it requires no additional reflectors to direct the light forwards .*

(LEFT) *At its simplest, accent lighting requires just a bulb and a shield to direct light.*

3 Task Lighting

Since most of our waking lives are spent performing some form of activity, it is a shame that we do not spend more care in lighting those activities well. Good task lighting improves visual clarity, prevents tiredness and helps focus the mind on the job. Around the home we need optimum task lighting in the kitchen, bathroom and study, in the living room (usually a multi-purpose room), and in the bedroom.

As with accent lighting, the fittings that provide task lighting should have integral reflectors, or lenses even, that throw the light in a particular direction. But the important difference between the two is that task lighting sources should never be seen. They should be mounted in opaque reflectors to eliminate glare completely (table lamps can be fitted with nearly opaque shades, particularly in bedrooms).

It is glare from bright visible sources that tires and distracts the eyes and makes it impossible for them to adjust to the level of light thrown onto the task itself. A perfect example of task lighting is the table-mounted Anglepoise lamp.

For activities such as working in the kitchen and using the bathroom, a general background level of ambient light is also desirable, to reduce shadows and help throw light into cupboards. For watching television or working at a

VDU, the task is self-illuminating, so only a strong background level of ambient light is necessary.

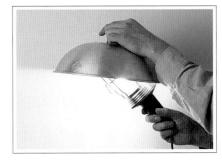

(ABOVE) *Any task light should have a reflective shield.*

(LEFT) *A crown-silvered bulb offers optimum task lighting. Unlike most reflector bulbs, there is no seepage of light behind or through the reflective coating.*

(BELOW) *Ceiling-mounted spots in this study give a non-glare supply of ambient light by being pointed away onto the wall. The keyboard is lit by a shielded tungsten striplight just above it.*

12

4 Decorative Lighting

Decorative lighting is selfish lighting; it says 'Look at Me'. At its simplest, it may be just the way a spotlight illuminates the coloured glass of some bottles and throws coloured shapes onto a surface. At its most extravagant, it is a highly decorative chandelier, or a neon sculpture. It is usually a deliberately contrived statement, to be seen as part of the entire decorative scheme of a room. Many architects and interior designers excel in such lighting.

But decorative lighting should also be used in conjunction with other lighting types, particularly ambient (which in the case of candle chandeliers, can provide a general unobserved background level). Because of its central role, decorative lighting becomes less effective if it has to compete with too much task or accent lighting; the schemes it occupies should rely on a discreet balance of elements.

This form of lighting also has an important psychological role to play. It should act as a unifier and focus for a room – a central fitting, if used in this way, must be dimmed to avoid any unflattering shadows from overhead – especially as it is often the crowning piece of whimsy in a decorative scheme.

(ABOVE) *A crown-silvered bulb can provide both decorative and ambient wall-lighting. See page 117 (No 3) for its integration into a decorative fitting.*

(LEFT) *A decorative shield over an ordinary bulb can still have a decorative effect.*

(BELOW) *A pendant like this can be seen simply as a skeletal frame on which you can build the trimmings of any decorative scheme.*

5 Kinetic Lighting

Hitherto, kinetic lighting has not really been recognized as a distinct type of lighting, but its peculiar characteristics merit a separate classification. As its name suggests, it is 'moving light'—the kind provided by candles or a real fire—and is a useful addition to any lighting scheme, except perhaps in a study.

But it is also the flickering light that jumps out from neon advertising hoardings and televisions. In many older houses fitted with central heating, it is the television which sits in the space formerly occupied by the fire. Here, the little flickering box in the corner of your eye starts to assume an ancient and powerful symbolism. A house does not seem alive, we are told, unless it has a flaming hearth – or the television switched on perhaps? In the 20th century, kinetic light from a television represents the centre of the homestead, just as the campfire did 5,000, and even 50,000, years ago.

Our household appliances are also touched with this living flame nowadays. LED displays wink and flash at us, the ghost in the machine mimicking the living flame.

And yet the most powerful and ritualistic use of kinetic light, in ancient and modern celebrations, does not exploit the high-tech, but the traditional: Hallowe'en lamps are fitted with candles; flaming torches light parades around the world; the church still relies on candlelight and incense plus stained glass and sunlight for its own brand of special effects; and we still marvel at fireworks.

Finally, the sun itself is the most dramatic form of kinetic light known to us. It is the ultimate living flame, the source of light and life. As it wheels daily through the sky, its shadows shift and move subtly, and heat-haze shimmers on the horizon. The weather systems it creates with its heat, produce wind and cloud which offer an infinite variety of moving light effects, both in the sky and on the ground.

It is the power, subtlety, beauty and sheer size of these constantly changing effects that have bewitched human beings for centuries. It is no small wonder that we crave and need even the merest flickering echo of them in our modern lives.

(ABOVE LEFT) *In this modern, minimal interior, kinetic light has been partly harnessed and subjugated. The fireplace is deep and recessed. But the scheme is nevertheless dominated by kinetic light from the television and natural daylight.*

(ABOVE) *Candlelight has for centuries represented the light of life.*

(BELOW) *Firelight offers kinetic light at its most traditional in a domestic setting.*

One Room Five Ways

To demonstrate clearly the five types of lighting that can be used in the home, we took an empty room and lit it using different combinations of the five types of light source.

This exercise shows lighting in its most naked form, but it does illustrate how a room's architecture can be flattered – or confused – by a lighting scheme. In the next part of the book you will find a case study for each room in the house; each of these is also lit in three different ways. For each case study you will find an analysis of the lighting, with marks on a scale of one to five for the amount of ambient, accent, task, decorative and kinetic light.

1 ACCENT ONLY

Without the combination of light and shadow we cannot see form; they are both necessary for us to make sense of the world. The naked bulb in this shot is a powerful 150-watt PAR lamp that has a reflector at the back to throw the light forward. The result is a room of strong contrast, using only accent lighting. Without any ambient lighting at all, even the shadows of the chair on the floor are inky black.

2 HIGH AMBIENT

An alabaster bowl takes the place of a downlighter to cast light in exactly the opposite direction; upwards onto the ceiling. The ceiling reflects the light like a large parabolic reflector and the result is a high level of ambient light which blankets the room – note how the shadow under the chair is soft and indistinct.

This lighting is good as a background to relaxing activities such as watching television. But used by itself, it needs an addition of sparkle and interest, since it tends to homogenize the room's features and architecture into a bland sameness. The wall sconces, although shaded, are only decorative, but provide welcome light relief to the scheme.

3 CANDLE GLOW

A much more intimate and decorative setting is achieved by adding candlelight. The wall lights have adopted a more assertive role in this setting by being fitted with bulbs of a higher wattage, while the central pendant bowl has been dimmed. Even the use of just a few dimmers in your home, together with separately organized circuits for your wall lights, table lamps and ceiling lights, will make a huge difference to the overall effect.

4 TASK AND ACCENT

Living rooms and dining rooms will benefit from a scheme composed primarily of directional spots. They can be mounted in the ceiling, or as here, on the walls and on the mantelpiece.

The latter choice gives you great flexibility because the lights are

(BELOW) 1: *Accent only*

(ABOVE) 2: *High ambient*

(ABOVE) 3: *Candle glow*

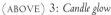

(ABOVE) 4: *Task and Accent*

(ABOVE) 5: *Sophisticated combination*

portable, can swivel, and can be plugged straight into an ordinary wall socket. Directional lights provide strongly contrasting lighting levels (hence the need to introduce some low-level decorative lighting in the centre of the room to add focus), and are best used to illuminate pictures, objects, sculptures and architectural features.

In libraries and studies choose a less jarring composition of background ambient light supplemented with bright close-up task lighting over the desk or workstation.

5 SOPHISTICATED COMBINATION

In reality most rooms serve many purposes and require a combination of lighting types; task lighting to read or work by; ambient background light to soften shadows, reduce contrast and make the environment more comfortable (it is provided here by the wall-mounted uplighters).

Decorative lighting fixtures such as chandeliers add focus and poise to decorative schemes, while directional accent lighting picks out features and objects in a room; the chemistry of these combinations will vary from room to room, according to the primary tasks that we perform in them.

Be Your Own
Lighting Designer

'May not the harmony and discord of Colours arise from the proportions of the Vibrations propagated through the fibre of the optick Nerves into the Brain, as the harmony and discords of Sounds arise from the proportions of the Vibrations of the Air? For some colours if they be view'd together are agreeable to one another, as those of Gold and Indigo, and others disagree.'
ISAAC NEWTON, *Opticks*, 1704

The easiest way to become a lighting designer is to go out and buy a safety lamp with an Edison-screw fitting like the one featured on page 8. It is the type of lamp used for inspecting car engines. Together with the kitchen utensils featured on pages 8-13, you can, with the help of a friend, approximate the five main types of lighting (see also pages 8-13) and experiment to see which arrangement suits you best. Once you have mastered this low-tech skill, you can progress by going on to use two more safety lamps and a collection of bulbs: a PAR 38 150-watt, 30-degrees floodlamp; two ISL lamps, one 60-watt, one 100-watt; two crown reflector bulbs (60 or 100 watt will do). Only the latter are available in bayonet fittings, so this is where your Edison-screw safety inspection lamps come in useful.

Using three inspection lamps hung from doors, picture hooks, or simply held in a friend's hand, you can begin to mock up an approximation of the lighting scheme you have planned. This is a relatively cheap but extremely effective way of finding out what you want. In addition, there is an ingenious little lamp which you should never be without; a small, moveable, low-voltage light with its own built-in transformer and switch that plugs straight into the mains to produce a bright, white light. One is shown on page 15, sitting on the mantelpiece. It can be placed behind furniture to wash walls; on fireplaces to uplight pictures or objects; on a shelf to downlight as task or accent lighting; or on the top of a cupboard to uplight a ceiling with ambient light. It will be the most versatile fitting you buy and proves the point that the lamp or fitting is just the start when designing lighting; the creative process is what you do with it.

MEASURING LIGHT

Before we can begin to understand how to measure light, it is important to understand something of what it is we are measuring. You will find a more detailed and scientific explanation of light and its frequencies on page 135. Light travels in straight lines, is filtered through the atmosphere and absorbed into every surface it hits. The remainder, which is reflected back onto our retinas, can often be only a fraction of that produced at source, so different calibrations are used to measure light at different points along its line of travel.

Put simply, we need to measure light not only at the point where it is produced, but also as it travels and once it has landed on, and reflected off, a surface. Only then can we estimate how much light we are going to need. The units of measurement are as follows:

CANDELA: Traditionally the brightness of one candle and the measure of Luminous Intensity. This is measured at source, right against the lamp, and is only really a useful tool for the lighting manufacturer or designer.

LUMEN: This is the unit of Luminous Flux, or flow of light, from any one source. One candle has a flow of about 12 lumens, while a new, clean 100-watt bulb produces 1200 lumens.

LUX: This is the measure of Illuminance, or the amount of light actually hitting a surface, ie lumens per square metre (yard). One lumen arriving at 1 square metre (yard) will register 1 lux. The further you are away from the light source, the more atmospheric pollution and interference will reduce the lux reading. In the USA, the term foot-candle is still used, which represents lumens per square foot.

HOW MUCH LIGHT?

If we want to know how bright a room should be, there are published guidelines as to the minimum illuminance levels for different human activites. A dim room should safely provide a reading of 50 lux, a kitchen should read 300 lux, an office 500-750 lux and a table top, where close work and accurate colour matching is needed (such as for needlework or antique restoration), 1000 lux. Activities such as electronic circuitry work, which calls for visual aids, need 1500-2000 lux.

To give you a rough measuring gauge, a low-voltage halogen spotlight fitted in a 3 m (10 ft) high ceiling with a 35-watt bulb will produce about 500 lux in the centre of its beam on the floor; a table top would be nearer to the source, so the lux level on it would be about double (1000 lux), in the centre of the beam. Towards the outside of

the beam, the lux level drops dramatically. This level of illuminance is about the same for a 100-watt PAR 38 spotlight, which is a conventional mainsvoltage, large tungsten spotlight.

You can take your own rough and ready lux readings using a camera with a built-in light meter. It should not be pointed at the light source, but close to a lit surface such as a wall or table top. Take care that neither you nor the camera cast a shadow on the surface. With the ASA set at 100 and the aperture set at f4, read off the shutter speed. 1/100th of a second gives you a reading of 1000 lux, 1/20th = 200 lux and so on. This method is about the only reliable way of ensuring that you are going to have enough light in a room, and it is best combined with the 'practice run' of setting up temporary lights which has already been explained.

But why go to all the fuss of buying

bulbs and using cameras when the manufacturers give the lumen reading on the lightbulb packet? You could, for example, try to calculate a rough lux level for the room by using this information and measuring the total number of square metres (yards) comprising the walls, floors and ceilings. There are two problems here, however. The first is that the light fittings you choose for a room may be very directional, like downlighting spotlights or table lamps, concentrating a high lux reading in one area. The other is the problem of reflectance. Different surfaces reflect differing amounts of light. A matt white-painted plaster wall will reflect 70 per cent of the light hitting it, absorbing the other 30 per cent, while a dark granite or stone floor will absorb a staggering 90 per cent of the light hitting it (see diagrams below left and overleaf).

REFLECTANCE

We see coloured surfaces as such only because, say, a red surface is one which absorbs every frequency of light, except red, which it bounces back onto our retinas. Consequently, since many of the frequencies are absorbed, a strongly coloured surface will reflect a very small percentage of the light hitting it. The problem of reflectance can be mildly improved by giving the material a gloss surface rather than a matt one. A gloss surface is really one which, under the microscope, has a very smooth surface (a matt one is broken up, so reflecting the light in all directions). It is, consequently, very efficient

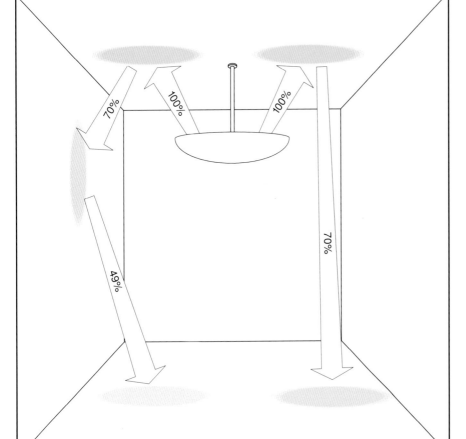

(LEFT) *Reflected light (1). The white walls and ceiling each absorb 30 per cent of the light. The floor receives a mixture of light reflected off the walls and off the ceiling and so is illuminated with between 49-70 per cent of the light it might receive if lit with an equally powerful floodlamp mounted in the ceiling, pointing down.*

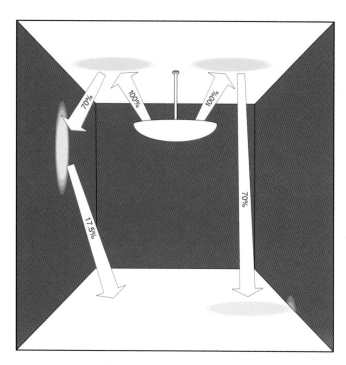

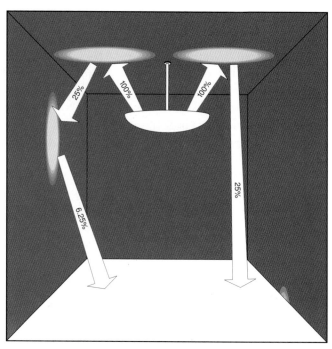

(ABOVE) *Reflected light (2). Where the walls are painted a dark colour, the floor receives between 17.5 and 70 per cent of what it would if lit by a downwards pointing floodlight of the same intensity as the uplighter.*

(ABOVE) *Reflected light (3). When the ceiling is also painted a dark colour, you can see that the lux readings go right down to a maximum of only 25 per cent.*

at reflecting any light hitting it straight back to the source. But most of us do not prefer a high gloss finish to our interior walls.

The illustration on the previous page shows what happens when a light source is mounted in an opaque ceiling uplighter in a white room. Because the light is reflected first off the ceiling and then off the wall, the eventual lux reading is much lower than say from a desk reading lamp, which is focusing all its lumens on one area without having to bounce the light off a surface.

LIGHT AND COLOUR
Just as we perceive shape and form from the light reflected by an object, so its colours are the frequencies of light that it reflects onto our retinas. From white sunlight, a red rose will absorb

every colour of the rainbow except red. What it rejects, we marvel at.

Consequently, if we shine a red light at the rose, it seems to vibrate with

colour, whereas a green light will turn it black. Because so many artificial lights are not pure white (see the chart on pages 136-39 for an analysis of dif-

(RIGHT) *Form, colour, texture and reflectance combine to inform us about our world. Far from requiring simple messages, our faculties are highly tuned to appreciate subtle and complex arrangements of these different qualities.*

ferent lights), colours can look vastly different under what are apparently very similar, whitish lights.

For example, the warm orange-red cast of tungsten lighting is ideal for lighting flesh tones, unlike many fluorescent lights, which emit huge quantities of magenta pink or green light in amongst their 'whitish' light.

It is important to look at the colour value of light in two ways; first in terms of its Colour Value, which is essentially an emotional reaction to the bulb colour when lit, and secondly its Colour Rendering, a more scientific term. There is a defined international system for measuring how effective light sources are at producing good colour rendering — in other words, imitating the colour of direct natural sunlight. At the moment the field is led by halogen, metal halide and some of the new 'cool' or 'colour corrected' fluorescent light bulbs.

As to the response of colours to different lights, there are without doubt some colours that react more strikingly to the diurnal change of light sources. The living room walls on page 38 are raspberry in cool blue daylight under a grey sky, but turn terracotta under tungsten.

A similarly interesting exercise is to take warm and cool variations of the same colour paints and colourwash each onto a wall, in layers. The result is an interesting surface that will change under differing lighting conditions. There are even some colours, 'cusp colours', that produce this effect when applied straight from the can. Examples of these include dark blue/purples, terracotta reds and pale blue/greens. As the names suggest, you can identify a cusp colour from its refusal to be classified as being exactly of one colour's stable.

LIGHT COMFORT

Another pitfall of poor lighting design is that of glare, when a light source is directly visible and so bright that the

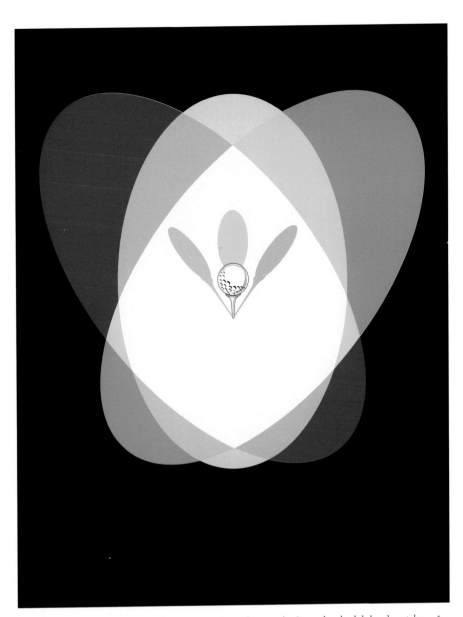

eye cannot accommodate both it and the effect it creates.

The simple mistake is to conclude that all light sources should be hidden from view, and that only their effect should be noticeable. This, however, ignores the psychological value of visible light sources as stimulants, attractants and reminders of more primitive and natural light sources around which we have built our lives for thousands of years; the sun, moon, and the flickering fireside.

The way to incorporate visible light sources into our interiors is to shield the source with larger diffusing shades of paper, frosted glass, parchment or

(ABOVE) *Science has decided that the rainbow of colours that make up pure white light can actually be reduced to three primary colours. But beware! These primaries are not quite the primary colours you may be used to when mixing paint, that is red, yellow and blue. They are instead red, green and blue, and by combining them in various ways, the other rainbow colours and pure white can be created.*

This diagram illustrates what happens when three spotlights, each coloured to represent one of the primaries, are shone onto a golfball sitting on a white background. For example, where green and red overlap they produce yellow light. This colour is also reproduced as one of the golf ball's shadows, which lies in an area lit by all three lamps, producing white light. The shadow is that cast by the blue lamp and so consists of the three primaries minus blue, ie red and green, making yellow.

other translucent materials (a frosted ordinary GLS bulb is the simplest example).

Or we can use small reflectors to diffuse the source, positioned around it or, as in the case of the crown-silvered

bulb, incorporated into the lamp.

Third, in the case of decorative fittings, we can dim the lighting by using a dimmer or by using low-wattage bulbs.

(ABOVE) *The highest-tech available: Absolute Action's 'infinity floor', a decorative installation made using mirrors and fibre optics.*

New Developments

Many lighting designers predict an introduction into the home market for fibre-optic lighting, which is now becoming popular in commercial and retail installations. As was the case with tungsten-halogen lighting, new developments take place in the commercial sector first and then filter down to you and me, the consumer.

Although fibre-optics give a clean, white and safe lighting source at the end of fibre-bundles, the light sources themselves are bulky at present and the whole system can also be extremely expensive.

But not so all those light sources that at the moment seem dangerous and unknown to us; metal halide, high-pressure sodium and mercury, and mains-voltage tungsten-halogen. Originally produced for industrial lighting fittings, these sources are now used in shops and offices. Although dangerous to dispose of because of their toxic metal contents, they produce a pleasant light to look at, and the first three are certainly very energy efficient.

Metal halide lighting is now used for many car headlamps, and although its colour rendering is excellent, its colour value is strange; when viewed directly it seems to sparkle with piercing flashes of green and purple light. The high-pressure sodium and mercury lamps which are now available are compact and give off respectively, yellowish and bluish casts of light. They can sometimes be seen together in sports halls and shopping malls, providing a mixed lighting colour to approximate something between the two of them.

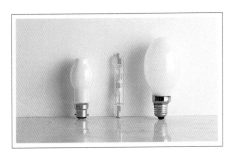

(ABOVE from left to right)
Mains-voltage halogen bulb producing good white light from a regular socket.

Metal halide tube and high pressure sodium bulb. Both of these sources are becoming increasingly available, together with high-pressure mercury sources in the form of tubes, bulbs or even reflector bulbs. However, they may require starting gear to be wired into a electrical circuit near them, and the materials used in them are highly dangerous.

The risk of explosion that early lamps suffered (producing showers of poisonous metals) has been overcome by strengthening the lamps, reducing their size and incorporating them into a double envelope of glass.

The one problem encountered with halide, mercury and sodium lights is that at the moment they need starting gear to warm them up, a process which can take minutes, and not something you are prepared to wait for when you walk into a room and switch on the light. But the equipment is becoming smaller and the 'striking time', as it is called, shorter. Even now, workshop and garage lighting is available in these sources on the retail market. Their incredible efficiency and therefore cheap running costs, will mean their inevitable introduction into the home market. Osram have already introduced

a discreet 15 x 3 cm (6 x 1 in) bulb onto the market for use in shops. It has both a mercury and a sodium source in one lamp, allowing the user to switch from one to the other.

The other interesting development is the widespread introduction of cheap, intelligent lighting systems; bulbs, sockets, plugs and remote controls that respond to simple instructions. The American Beacon Company have produced a tungsten bulb that requires no special wiring, responding simply to how many times it is switched on and off. It has four levels of brightness, a fifth lowest level as a nightlight, which it reduces to over 20 minutes; a flashing 'emergency' function; and a built-in 'off' button that can be set to any length of time. All this tiny electronic wizardry, that just plugs into the lighting socket, even saves energy and lasts twice as long as ordinary bulbs.

Without doubt, most of today's research money in the lighting industry is being spent on developing fluorescent lighting that gives an even, white light without the nasty 'spikes' it has always had. The big manufacturing companies like Philips already have one or two rather good products on the market. Ultimately they will provide offices, workshops and homes with a dimmable cool white, almost daylight quality light that does not distort colours.

Rather than less fluorescent lighting in our homes, we will probably see more, in increasingly compact and unusual forms.

Chapter I

THE HALLWAY

The difficulty lies in distributing the light in such a manner that certain parts appear particularly bright, whilst others are subduedly lit, and others again are in complete shadow. Just as the painter works with blended tones and shadow in his pictures, so the lighting engineer should learn to adopt these lighting techniques.

THE BALLET MASTER,
JEAN GEORGES NOVERRE
(1760)

A hallway can be lit in any number of ways, depending on its size and major features. But perhaps the most important requisite is that the lighting should be warm and welcoming. This hall is in an 18th-century house which was first an inn and then an orphanage.

While this space is particularly bright, because of an internal glazed door with a window behind it, many hallways will not have all these features. Most of the lighting tricks shown here, however, can be adapted to suit darker and smaller spaces.

(LEFT)
A table lamp in a hallway gives a very welcoming light, whatever the time of day or night.

The Hallway

(BELOW) *The parchment covered door leading into the kitchen makes the light coming into the hallway incredibly warm.*

DAYLIGHT

The use of a glazed door into the kitchen below allows the room to be filled with natural light from a south-facing window. In this instance, the sunlight has been modified by the use of lining wallpaper soaked in linseed oil and wired to the glazing bars across the window.

This technique is based on the 17th-century Dutch tradition of using paper dipped in linseed oil and then fastened to small, individual folding timber frames to become mini-shutters. The paper is tough, waterproof and translucent. Once oiled, it takes on the appearance of rough parchment. It is the perfect filter for sun-

Ratings:
Ambient: 5
Task: 0
Kinetic: 3 (moving leaves)
Decorative: 3
Accent: 0

(ABOVE) *A warm evening welcome is created by using this table lamp.*

Ratings:
Ambient: 0
Accent: 5
Task: 0
Kinetic: 2
Decorative: 4

light, which it transforms into a brown, subtle and warm light. There is no need to cover all the frames in a window, just use enough to screen the sunlight, or to give the room the privacy you need.

NIGHT-TIME

Late at night, the use of one or more table lamps with shades made from the same oiled paper, transform the hallway (above left) into a cosy reception room. Table lamps give local light at eye-level, which is shielded. Consequently, they will always give a room an intimate, almost festive feel. Their light acts on a psychological level, drawing people inwards; it has the same effect as the flames of a fire or candle, used to good effect further down the hall. Table lamp light is the perfect accompaniment to a fire and helps to create the welcoming atmosphere essential for a hall.

Lamps with small bases are extremely versatile and can be used in a variety of places, such as on mantel-

pieces or in alcoves where they successfully uplight the ceiling.

GENERAL LIGHT

Hallways, like other rooms in the house, benefit from the use of ambient lighting. A good, general background light is provided above right by two wall-mounted Gothic uplighters, each containing a 100-watt, mains-voltage halogen tube. They are both wired to a dimmer switch and, as with all types of ambient lighting, there is no obvious light source and no glare. The room is bathed in an even cast of relaxing light, which provides a reasonably high level of illumination from an inconspicuous source.

Ambient lighting is ideal because it serves as the general base level of lighting into which other types of lighting can be added. Here a small decorative ceiling light adds a twinkle. For a different and more generalized lighting effect, uplight the ceiling from a hanging opaque pendant in the middle.

(ABOVE) *Uplighters successfully light a hallway without glaring the passer-by.*

Ratings
Ambient: 5
Accent: 0
Task: 0
Kinetic: 0
Decorative: 1

Details and Tricks

DECORATIVE LIGHT

This stairwell illustrates how much interest can be added to a decorative scheme by exploiting very direct sources of light to create shadows and patterns. The wall is painted white which under an ambient source would seem dull and flat. But here a decora-tive lantern produces dramatic effects. Its open metal framework cladding the bulb produces shadows all around it, and these are sharpened by the use of a naked, clear bulb. A frosted or pearl bulb would produce softer shadows since the smaller the light source is, the sharper the shadows it produces. An even softer effect could have been produced by installing a filter of paper or silk into the frame of the lantern, effectively turning it into a lampshade.

By day, natural light from a landing window produces more interest on the wall by casting shadows from a balustrade. Note the difference in colour between the warm light of the tungsten bulb and the bluish-grey cast of the daylight.

FILTERED LIGHT
Sunlight (below right), when filtered through the oiled lining paper, takes on a much creamier cast, producing softer shadows.

Compare this to the photograph below left, where, without the paper filter, the pot is lit by the typical natural light of an overcast day. In the northern hemisphere, grey skies give a very blue cast of light (not pure white light, as is generally assumed), while Mediterranean light is much whiter.

Technically, the colour of light is measured by the Kelvin temperature chart of light, and northern grey daylight measures between 7000 and 8000 degrees (for temperatures of all types of light see page 135).

CHECKLIST

* The hallway can be lit in any way with any type of lighting.

* Lighting inside a hallway should help to create a warm, welcoming atmosphere.

* Consider security lighting for porches and outdoor safety lighting that automatically switches on when triggered by movement or body heat.

(BELOW)
Natural light

(BELOW)
Filtered light

Planning the Light

The hallway is the corridor between us and the outside world, the airlock that smoothes the passage from our cocooned domestic environment to the harsher surroundings beyond. And, of course, it performs the reverse function, welcoming us into the intimacy of the homestead. It is often impossible to squeeze even one piece of furniture in

but they become altogether more cheery places for having light not only at the end of them, but also dotted along them.

The hall is a place of transition, and its lighting should gently accommodate the eye to different levels of brightness. If your hall is dark by day, then install a bright ambient source such as a powerful uplighter, to mimic daylight. But do make sure to dim it in the evening

to give your eyes a chance to become accustomed to the dark outside.

CEILINGS: THE UNUSED SPACE

Table lamps, lamp stands and even wall lights frequently can't be used in hallways because of the space limitations. But inspiration can come from above.

The room above shows a complicated arrangement of decorative and task

lighting using exclusively low-voltage halogen fittings in dichroic reflectors. The sheer number of these means that they highlight nothing in particular. Instead they act as wallwashers and so are really a source of ambient light. The blue room (above), however, relies on unashamedly industrial fittings to do nothing but provide ambient light, using the ceiling as a giant reflector, offering the same shadowless light as provided by a cloudy sky.

If your home is of historical value and should suffer minimum damage, or you are worried about the fire risk of installing downlighters into your ceiling, consider building a suspended timber platform into which the fittings can be mounted (top right).

One treatment for an historically sensitive room is to use uplighting as shown to the right on the stair stringer. It should be diffused through filters to prevent glare when looking down from above.

(ABOVE AND TOP RIGHT) *Dimmers are really necessary with these fittings to adjust the setting according to the time of day.*

(RIGHT) *If possible, let the natural light in. This lantern floods the space below, and at night halogen uplighters light up the ceiling.*

(OPPOSITE) *This kind of arrangement would require two circuits, one for the chandelier-style arrangement of arms in the middle of the room, and one for the functional downlighters.*

(ABOVE) *Keep a*
chandelier like this
dimmed or fitted with
low-wattage bulbs to
avoid glare. And rely
on a secondary source
of lighting as backup.

CREATING DRAMA

In a survey conducted in the mid-1980s for a paint manufacturer, the researchers concluded – not unsurprisingly – that most people's preferred colour for the hallway was green; a choice suggesting the need to bring the outside in. The lighting implications of that are that we should light our halls with bright ambient light sources in order to mimic natural daylight. But, in practice, most people prefer to take a more delicate and subtle approach, combining the need for bright exterior safety lighting with interior decorative and accent lighting.

This is sensible; first, because during the day enough natural light usually comes into the hall through glazed panels in the front door or surround; and second, because in the evening the hall is a place of welcome for the guest. It is their first taste of hospitality, and so should gently lead into the artificially lit interior of the house.

However, the hallway and the stairway are places where lighting can be used to great dramatic effect, as the first welcoming gesture of hospitality and of the theatre of entertaining, as the picture above right shows.

Likewise, the chandelier above left

shows just how integrated a decorative fitting can become. A stairwell is the perfect setting for a showy piece like this one, whether it is traditional or contemporary, because it acts as a focus for the space and allows us to travel up and around it, getting a full and complete view.

(ABOVE) *In restricted spaces we can find ourselves on very intimate terms with a light fitting - sometimes we are never far from a wall or ceiling.*

Chapter 2

THE LIVING ROOM

Steps must be taken to ensure that daylight brightness or lamp brightness is not only toned down, but concentrated on particular spots and kept away from others — in short, that it is properly distributed in the daytime, this is done with the help of curtains and sun blinds, and at night, with the help of various types of lighting screens.

HENRY HARVARD, L'ART DANS LA MAISON (1884)

In terms of leisure activities the living room is perhaps the most versatile room in the house. We entertain friends, watch television, read, listen to music and relax here, so any lighting plan should cater for all these functions.

Interior lighting at its best utilizes and enhances the major decorative and architectural features of a room and its contents. In this living room there is a dark ceiling, so the white walls, rather than the ceiling, perform the job of a giant reflector. This function has been exploited in each of the lighting schemes shown here. The walls are lit with different-coloured lights and the furniture, pictures and ornaments used as props in creating different moods and decorative embellishments in what is, essentially, a plain white unadorned box.

(LEFT)
Coloured uplighters at the back of the shelves throw the decorative ornaments into dramatic - and colourful - relief.

Psychedelic Colour

REST AND RELAXATION

By lighting the walls with creamy, soft tone bulbs in a central fitting and various spotlights around the room, the space is washed and united by a single colour. The yellowy-white cast of the light is nearly all reflected off the walls to give a high level of ambient light. This provides a warm, relaxed, friendly atmosphere which is conducive to relaxing in front of the television or talking late into the night. The strong colours of the furniture are also muted in this light and their presence subjugated to the room's overall character. The fire is a strong source of lively light.

(BELOW) The brightly lit ornaments in the corner of the living room give a focal point to an otherwise generally lit room.

Ratings:
Ambient: 4
Accent: 5
Task: 0
Decorative: 2
Kinetic: 4

(ABOVE)
The ideal lighting for a drinks party: subtle and yet colourful. The seating has not been lit to avoid glare for anyone choosing to sit down.

Ratings:
Ambient: 2
Accent: 4
Task: 2
Decorative: 2
Kinetic: 3

GLOWING VASES

If lighting is applied to one particular area of a room, it will focus the eye and provide a point of interest. In the room to the left, the glass vases to the right of the fireplace are lit from behind with ordinary pygmy tungsten bulbs. The bright white glow which emanates from the vases mirrors the light produced by the real fire.

DRINKS PARTY

To create a party atmosphere, low-level coloured lighting is used above left. The central overhead light has been switched off, while the spotlights around the room have been fitted with red, blue and yellow bulbs. These colours are reflected on the white walls all around the room. For a successful evening lighting scheme it is important to use lighting that complements the room's design and contents. This psychedelic scheme perfectly matches the 1970s' Italian furniture.

Glass ornaments are illuminated from behind by bulbs of the same colour to produce powerful and large shadows. The great advantage of using coloured bulbs is that when their

reflected light mixes, a brand new colour is created. Here the blue and red lights have fused to produce mauve.

The floor is highlighted by a soft, white light cast by a flood lamp turned down low, which, along with the fire, ensures that the room still retains its charm and warmth. For parties, chairs and sofas should not be highlighted, as anyone who sits on them will be lit unflatteringly by a glaring and disconcerting light.

LATE NIGHT

For a more dramatic effect the lights previously reflected on the wall have been dimmed, making the edges of the room disappear. Instead, parts of the floor and furniture have been spotlit like actors on a stage, thereby drawing attention to the colours, form and texture of the furniture.

The possible starkness of the room has been counteracted by the warm, moving light of the fire and the glow from the orange and red vases. Lit from behind, they look like small table lamps and throw splashes of colour around the room.

(ABOVE) *For a more intimate atmosphere the lighting is focused on the centre of the room, leaving the perimeters in darkness.*

Ratings:
Ambient: 0
Accent: 5
Task: 0
Decorative: 3
Kinetic: 4

(RIGHT)
Mini spotlights

Details and Tricks

MINI SPOTLIGHTS

Imaginative but simple lighting can make all the difference to a room. The lemons above become an unusual centrepiece when lit by three mini halogen spotlights. The lamps are sold as part of a kit which includes wires and glass shelves. A discreet metal strip which powers the 12-volt lamps runs along the shelf, gathering a low voltage from the wires supporting the shelf.

MULTI-COLOURED LIGHTS

A simple way of creating exciting lighting is to mount coloured bulbs in small holders and hide them behind and between ornaments. Floor-or table-mounted halogen uplighters are ideal for this. (Always allow plenty of air gaps for heat to escape and do not place bulbs near flammable materials.) The result is dramatic shadows and patterns which mingle together like the mixed colours on an artist's paint palette. Primary colours also fuse together to form a rainbow of secondary colours.

REFLECTOR SPOTLIGHTS

A silver-backed tungsten bulb spotlight reflector is a conventional 1960s design (see opposite, top). An alternative design incorporates a crown-silvered reflector bulb which directs the light into a wider reflector on the fitting.

FRAMING PROJECTOR

A framing projector, a complicated arrangement of low-voltage halogen light and lenses, is discreetly mounted in the ceiling (see page 61) and focused onto the masks (below). The beam of light is slightly larger than the masks and is softly focused, giving the impression of a halo. It is perfectly possible to give the beam an intricate profile and a hard edge.

COWL LIGHT

The shelf light below looks like a theatre prompt box and includes a cowl (or half tube) with a low-voltage capsule inside. Although small, it has a considerable effect, throwing powerful shadows onto the wall, making a sharp line of light reflected in each glass.

(ABOVE) *Reflector spotlights*

CHECKLIST

* The living room, with its many functions, is best served by a wide variety of lighting. Use several different circuits with dimmer switches.

* Provide decorative lighting for entertaining. This could be as simple as replacing ordinary tungsten bulbs with coloured versions.

* Make sure there is enough ambient lighting for relaxing, listening to music or watching television in the form of spotlights, concealed lighting or wall uplighters.

* Consider mixing tungsten and halogen lighting in order to provide alternative 'warm' and 'cool' settings.

(BELOW) *Masks lit by a framing projector*

(BELOW) *Cowl light*

Planning the Light

The way in which a room's colour scheme is lit is as important as choosing the colours themselves. Lighting can subdue colour or it can impregnate a whole room with various shades of the main colour. If wall colours are not to dominate a room, the ceiling should be painted in a correspondingly paler or neutral colour and also carefully uplit to provide a good level of colourless ambient light.

Wall lights should be avoided because they turn wall space into a giant reflector, which intensifies the colour in the room. If, on the other hand, you want the objects in a room to be cast in the same colour as the walls, then the ceiling should be painted with the same colour. Within this one-colour cast of light, separate objects and colours can be picked out with accent lighting.

You will also need to think about the style and colour of your furnishings. For example, if you have terracotta walls and heavy wooden pieces of furniture, you would need a white ceiling and bright accent lighting.

For an interesting effect, consider using colours that respond dramatically to the change that occurs between natural daylight and artificial tungsten light. Cusp colours, those that sit on the edge between one colour and another, are best for this. For example, a greying verdigris colour, which is bluish in daylight, turns green under a tungsten light.

(ABOVE) *This living room, in the house of architect Frank Lloyd Wright, is an excellent example of a totally integrated lighting system. The maximum level of daylight is obtained from the windows: a lighting trough provides a gentle uplight for the ceiling, and the lights incorporated into two brick structures discreetly redefine the architecture of the room, while remaining unobtrusive.*

(OPPOSITE) *The combination of natural and artificial lighting in this living room illustrates how light has the power to change the colours of a decorative scheme. When illuminated by daylight, the lit wall appears to be raspberry pink. But at night-time the yellowish light cast from the tungsten spotlight and floodlamp infuse it with tones of burnt sienna.*

(ABOVE AND TOP RIGHT) *Light sources can either be subtle and hidden, as in the picture above, or overtly obvious, making a staement, as in the chandelier top right.*

HIDDEN SOURCES

If lighting is to be hidden, there are various ways to make it dramatic, as shown to the left. A thin sliver of daylight from a concealed window provides an interesting effect, as do the three mains voltage halogen bulbs which are positioned low, downlighting the surrounding pale limestone. They are not, as would appear, providing accent or task light, but ambient. They are an unseen light source, which, by reflecting in the floor, helps to light up the room.

UNUSUAL FITTINGS

In an old house, the first choices for lighting solutions are antique or reproduction traditional fittings. However, modern fittings should not be dismissed either. When practical lighting is needed, the simple solution appears to be a functional lamp. But the examples above and overleaf on page 42 show that there is no reason why you cannot use a more unusual lamp in a different context. Don't be afraid to use lamps and lighting fittings as decorative statements in their own right.

The lighting in the room above, for example, is a surprise because chandeliers are usually hung low only over dining room tables. But a fitting like this can be an interesting decorative object, providing a focus for the room when hung low over a coffee table or a sideboard. In this case, the table obviously stops anyone bumping into it.

There are three advantages to using a chandelier in this way: first there is no need for a high level of lighting because the chandelier is local to any activity, so acts as a kind of task light; second, by being hung low the candles are easily accessible; and finally, the light output can be backed up by other lighting in the ceiling without detrimentally affecting the aesthetic appeal of the piece.

(ABOVE) *The overall effect of this umbrella lamp is that of a glowing object against a glowing wall with a light that is evenly spread, providing the room with both decorative and ambient lighting.*

It would be easy to dismiss the umbrella lamp in the photograph above as showy or inappropriate. However, on closer inspection it proves to be a very apt source of light for the room. The light source itself, the bulb, is not facing directly onto the wall as this would produce a hotspot. Instead, the light is reflected three times: directly onto the silvered back of the bulb, then onto the umbrella which spreads and reflects the light onto the wall. In turn, the wall then distributes the light even further.

INCORPORATED LIGHTING

If you are planning to have an incorporated lighting scheme in the living room, you should measure how much natural light there is and assess the size, style and architecture of the room. Incorporated lighting is not just a matter of hiding a few lights or recessing them in surrounding structures, it needs to work with, and emphasize the architecture of, the room at all times of the day.

The living room is used for many different purposes during the course of a day, so its lighting scheme needs careful attention, as in the photograph to the right.

If possible, the lighting should be planned at the same time as other major decorative work. If you are re-decorating to the extent of stripping off wallpaper, think about the advantages of installing new or additional wall lights and ceiling fittings. The style, space and architecture of the room should also be considered when planning the lighting; think about the colour of the room and whether you want this to be a dominant feature or not, then try to choose light fittings that match or contrast with the style of the room.

Nowadays there is an an enormous range of light fittings to choose from - dimmers, downlights, uplights, accents, spotlights, etc. – and these should, in some way, complement the style of your furniture and decoration. The lighting should provide a level of flexibility, so it can be used in combination or in isolation. There should be lighting for emphasis on focal points, such as fireplaces and treasured objects; while areas used for different activities - reading or eating for instance — should be well lit.

(ABOVE) *This room includes a complex lighting arrangement. Plenty of daylight pours through the window and skylight, and the artificial lighting has been carefully planned to include a number of recessed halogen spotlights. These fittings highlight the books and ornaments. In addition, low-voltage halogen spotlights are focused onto the sofa from the edge of the gallery, producing both ambient and task lighting.*

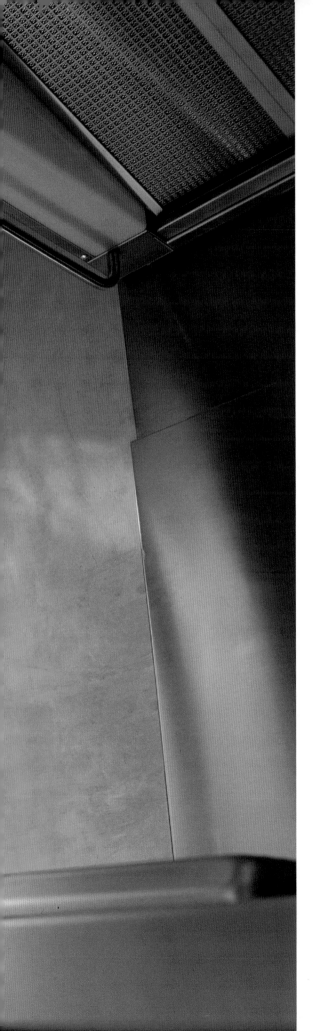

Chapter 3

THE KITCHEN

*The apothecaries and materialistics display
glasses ... filled with brightly coloured spirits, and
envelop entire quadratures in reddish-purple, yellow, verdigris,
and sky-blue light. The pastry cooks dazzle the eye with their
chandeliers and tickle the nose with their toppings.*

GEORG CHRISTOPH LICHTENBERG (1775)

In a kitchen the lighting has to look more than
just attractive, since it must also highlight and
emphasize various work activities. Subtle lighting may be great for dining by, but it is hope-
less if you are trying to peel a potato, heat the
soup, or wash up.

It is possible, however, to start with a functional lighting scheme and to add decorative
lighting gradually, as this modern galley
kitchen shows. The lighting scheme is achieved
by minimal effort, simply by switching off
some lights and switching on others, by using
light from appliances and by bouncing sources
of light off numerous kitchen objects.

(LEFT)
*Whatever the time of day, a kitchen needs to be well lit,
particularly at the work areas.*

Reflective Steel

DAYBREAK

During the day, this kitchen is infused with natural light which pours in through the large picture window, patio doors and skylight. The outside wall is painted white to further reflect natural light. The room is consequently very bright and cheerful.

The kitchen layout has been planned so that, wherever possible, task lighting is provided by a natural source, such as that received from the skylight for the chopping board.

Even if natural light is at a minimum, low-voltage halogen spotlights can highlight the areas which other lights cannot reach, as here, in the dark right-hand corner of the room.

In any lighting scheme, it is not only the lights that are important, but also the use of the room's inanimate objects. Part of this kitchen's charm lies in how light is bounced around the room by reflections and refractions in the glass shelves, the floor's glazed green slate, the slightly translucent plaster and the stainless steel units and sink. Even the polished chrome taps and kettle are part of the effect, exploding with reflected light.

Ratings:
Ambient: 5
Accent: 1 (corner)
Task: 5
Decorative: 0
Kinetic: 0

(BELOW) *A kitchen filled with light is a marvellous place to cook and eat in.*

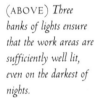

(ABOVE) *Three banks of lights ensure that the work areas are sufficiently well lit, even on the darkest of nights.*

Ratings:
Ambient: 3
Accent: 0
Task: 5 :
Decorative: 0
Kinetic: 0

SPACE STATION/ WORK STATION

At night this kitchen (above left) takes on a futuristic feel, with every one of its lights ablaze, like a culinary space station. The glass surfaces become mirrors, reflecting and bouncing light backwards. Task lighting is provided by three separate banks of light. On the left-hand side they cover the oven, fridge, cupboards and chopping board. On the right-hand side they focus on the sink, worktop, hob and kettle. The middle bank throws light over the floor which reflects it back into the cupboards when they are opened.

The extra-terrestrial feel of the kitchen is further enhanced by the green hue cast from the light of the hob. Again, the taps and the kettle offer extra effect by reflecting light onto the wall, creating a pattern at the top left-hand corner of the window.

DINING IN

As mentioned earlier, subtle lighting is much better for dining by, whether in the kitchen or in an adjacent room as shown here (above right). Merely by switching off a few lights and plugging in a couple of lamps, the kitchen has become a different room. The right-hand bank of lights focused on the sink are replaced by two table lamps. The resulting light is more subtle; table lamps bring people nearer to a light source which, when shaded, gives the psychological effect of sitting near a warm flame.

The table lamps also throw interesting shadows onto the wall through the glass shelves. The lighting peppers the kitchen with numerous spots of light that are bounced off the highly reflective surfaces.

One easy, but magical, effect can be created by angling a halogen spotlight to project through coloured storage bottles and jars. Small pools of coloured light fall onto the cupboards and green floor and are mirrored in the window and doors. This all contributes to making the kitchen, as an ancilliary area, a considerably more intimate and decorative setting for a dinner party.

(ABOVE) *For a more intimate atmosphere, try using table lamps in the kitchen. They offer a warmth far more conducive to a supper party than halogen lighting can supply.*

Ratings:
Ambient: 0
Accent: 5
Task: 1
Decorative: 4
Kinetic: 0

(ABOVE) *Kettle*

(ABOVE CENTRE)
Cupboard door

(ABOVE RIGHT)
Bottles

Details and Tricks

KETTLE

Any metal surface can be utilized to reflect light. Here the kettle and utensils throw out not only sparkles of light but also shadows into the room.

BOTTLES

Storage bottles and jars which are useful for holding anything from oil and vinegar to beans and dried fruits, are a cheap and effective way of reflecting and refracting coloured light when lit from behind.

CUPBOARD DOOR

A stainless steel surface often looks cold, but warm lighting can counteract this. The cupboard door (above centre) reflects two sources of halogen light: the dramatic streaking comes from a ceiling-mounted spotlight, the yellow patch is a reflection of an area of the plaster ceiling, uplit by the light that bounces off the draining board.

(RIGHT) *Wall light*

WALL LIGHT

The wall light in the adjacent dining area (below left) throws light up onto the ceiling to create a pink ambient glow. This is complementary to the task downlighting in the work areas.

RIPPLE GLASS SHELF

As this kitchen shows, glass is an excellent medium to help lighting come alive. Here (opposite, below left), the ripple glass shelf holding glass jars is lit by a halogen light above and to the right. Colour is bounced onto the ceiling and refracted on the wall. The halogen focused on the knife rack creates a dramatic shadow that tungsten spotlights cannot achieve, as their light source is too general.

SWITCHES

The top three switches in the picture opposite operate the three banks of light in the kitchen. The bottom three are for exterior lamps. It is possible to use dimmer switches in a kitchen, but they best serve environments with decorative lighting, and a kitchen's lighting is primarily functional. If the light is too bright, it is easier to replace halogen capsules with lower wattage ones, but check ceiling fittings and transformers to make sure you do not install a capsule of too high a wattage.

TABLE LAMP

When installing a table lamp, think about whether its design is sympathetic to the rest of the room. The lamp right has a low-voltage halogen bulb with green glass slats to complement the kitchen shelves. The lamp is not too bright, as the glass has an etched pattern that breaks up the light and creates a pattern on the wall.

HALOGEN SPOTLIGHT

It is not difficult to adapt lighting in the kitchen for different purposes. First, although a halogen light is more expensive compared to a GLS 40-watt tungsten bulb, its scope makes it a much better source of light, being whiter, brighter and easily directable. This superior type of halogen light

(LEFT) *Table lamp*

(below right) is held in a frame which is 5cm (2in) behind the ceiling surface. The access hole is 7.5cm (3in) wide and is covered by a small magnetic plate which can be painted the same colour as the ceiling.

With the capsule hidden in the ceiling, all you see is a glowing, warm area. This is far preferable to a bright, piercing light that invariably attracts your attention.

CHECKLIST

* A kitchen requires both task and ambient lighting which can be produced by the same lights or from a variety of light sources.

* Spotlights can create both functional and background lighting.

* Even the light that is bounced up off the floor from lights on the ceiling help to illuminate the inside of cupboards.

* If the kitchen is to be used for dining then it is easy to add decorative lighting.

(BELOW CENTRE)
Switches

(BELOW) *Ripple glass shelf*

(BELOW) *Halogen spotlight*

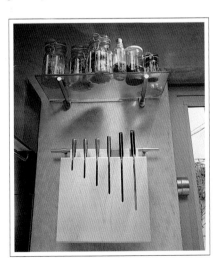

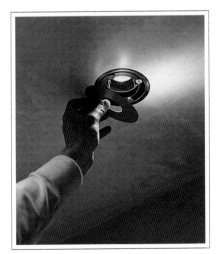

Planning the Light

Both ambient and task lighting are essential for a kitchen. They should provide a variety of different light sources to cater for the many activities which take place there, such as food-preparation, cooking and eating.

A well-considered scheme should include spotlights for oven and hob, directional lights for worksurfaces (such as recessed cupboard lights) and overhead lights for table or laundry area. The most versatile lighting can best be provided by low-voltage halogen spotlights.

(LEFT) Natural daylight provides both ambient and task lighting. The windows and the skylight above the worktops supply overall background light as well as illuminating the work areas.

You can capitalize on any natural light by positioning sinks and work-surfaces close to windows; darker rooms will need a greater combination of lighting options to work well. Think about ways of providing lighting for eating while leaving food prepara-tion areas in darkness once the cooking is finished.

AMBIENT AND TASK LIGHTING

As the two photographs opposite and above, and the one on page 52 show, there are several ways in which task and ambient lighting can be combined without detracting from the aesthetics of the kitchen.

In the photograph opposite, the eight industrial lights placed around the skylight (and again, over the worktops) provide ambient and task lighting in the

(ABOVE) The two low-hanging lampshades in this kitchen cleverly provide task and ambient lighting simultaneously.

(ABOVE) *Note how the lights' reflections in the surrounding metal surfaces help to make the setting much more decorative.*

following way. The lights' hollophane shades, which complement the kitchen's modern architecture, are of cast glass, ribbed on both sides. These ribs act rather like a lens, fracturing the light source to create a diffused, ambient light. Meanwhile, the bulbs within offer a high level of functional overhead task lighting.

A similar but less exciting effect can be achieved with the use of a much simpler and less expensive lamp. On page 51, two large pressed steel lampshades hover over the tables, providing task lighting to work and eat by. However, the expanse of the white underside of the shades reflects such broad patches of light (similar to those given off by a floodlamp) that the room is provided with its ambient lighting too.

Task and ambient lighting can, of course, be separated, but keep in mind the overall design of the room. Functional lighting does not have to mean unattractive or uninteresting fittings. In this room above, ambient light comes from the lighting behind the wall which uplights the ceiling with a dramatic, yellow light. Not only is this a strong theatrical effect, it makes the kitchen look more decorative too. A smaller but similar effect comes from the small wall light.

Practical downlighting is housed in the metal beam hung just above the worktop, but these lights are not just functional. They are controlled by a dimmer switch and can, when turned down low, produce a glowing, red light that is ideal for dining.

STYLE AND FUNCTION

When you are planning a kitchen lighting scheme, you should be very wary of placing style above function. With careful thought, it is perfectly possible to combine the two. The first of the following examples, above, illustrates the problem when an obsession with style takes over from functional requirements. The second, on page 54, shows lighting that caters for both sides of the equation but without too much imagination, and the final kitchen, on page 55, shows lighting which is a perfect combination, both stylistically and practically.

If you have a dark colour scheme, extra lighting will be needed because of the amount of light absorbed by the dark surfaces (see Reflectance, pages 17-18). This is, of course, particularly important in a kitchen, where you need to move around from one area to another as you cook, take food from cupboards and so on. Here (above), the kitchen's slate grey wall makes the room extremely dark, yet little has been done to alleviate the problem in the form of extra lighting. Although the one light above the worktop and sink provides strong task lighting and takes advantage of the light reflecting on the pale surface below, there is no ambient light to aid movement around the room and for lighting into cupboards.

The room may look good stylistically but this is an unhappy arrangement, with the kitchen in desperate need of more ambient light and more task lighting.

(ABOVE) *When planning the lighting in any room, but especially in a kitchen, it is essential to counteract the room's natural darkness. If possible, pale surfaces should be utilized to reflect the light up.*

(ABOVE) *The visible recessed spotlight above the window in this kitchen highlights the sink and supplants daylight in the evening.*

The kitchen (above) shows how to create a well-lit kitchen which is both classically designed and functional, even if it is a little on the conservative side. The lighting is incorporated into the kitchen's fittings and colour scheme. Unlike the previous example, there is no danger here of the green surfaces rendering the room darker. Plenty of task lighting is provided by two ceiling lights and by lamps sited beneath the plinth of the wall cupboards. The fact that these lights are hidden, throwing light across the floor, means they also provide some ambient light.

Of the three examples shown on page 53, above and opposite, the kitchen opposite is the most successful. A lot of thought has gone into providing lighting for the many functions of

the kitchen, while also remaining empathetic to the room's overall design. The best lighting arrangement in a kitchen is to install a number of different types of light and to control them with dimmer switches.

The lighting trough along the left-hand side of the kitchen above holds both uplighting, in the form of three mains voltage halogen tubes, and downlighting, by means of a row of six recessed, low-voltage halogen spotlights.

The trough provides ambient, task and decorative lighting for all kitchen activities. Three attractive and durable storm lanterns are hung in the centre of the room and in the evening their tungsten bulbs provide a decorative, soft yellow light.

(ABOVE) *Here the repeated lines of lights in sixes and threes add an aesthetic geometry to the room. The use of the installed 'trough' means that the traditional architecture of the ceiling can remain uncluttered.*

Chapter 4

THE DINING ROOM

I think the nightlife of society a hundred years since was rather a dark life. There was not one wax candle for then which we now see in a lady's drawing room. Horrible guttering tallow smoked and stunk in passages ... bless Mr Price and Luciferous benefactors of mankind for banishing the abominable mutton of our youth.

THACKERAY,
THE VIRGINIANS

The dining room is, apart from the living room, the main room in the house for entertaining. At other times the room may be used for reading, having tea and playing with the children. The lighting should therefore be conducive to conversation, flattering to diners but also bright for practical uses. All these similar but subtly different functions mean that dining room lighting has to be planned around a number of different types of lights. The room in our case study has a lighting system programmed for different settings by a Leax control switch (see Details, page 60). A cheaper solution can be created with a combination of bulbs and dimmer switches.

(LEFT)
Careful lighting of ornaments makes them an item of focal attention.

58

Mood Dining

DINNER FOR TWO

For a romantic dinner for two, lighting should be soft and intimate, warm and seductive. Candles and candelabras are the obvious choice for such an occasion.

To draw the room in and concentrate on the two dining places, a chandelier with a rise and fall mechanism has been hung low over the table and the light from the bulbs turned down low. Complementary lighting comes from the candles on the side table.

A chandelier can be powered by electricity or by candles, but a useful trick is to have one that is mixed. Where bulbs and candles alternate the bulbs can be turned up full when complete illumination is needed and turned down low for dinner parties, matching the light strength of the candles. If clear bulbs are used, they reflect the candle flames and make the chandelier appear to be candlelit only.

Ratings:
Ambient: 0
Accent: 5
Task: 2
Decorative: 5
Kinetic: 3

(BELOW) Create a romantic setting by using candlelight – here they are used both in the chandelier and on the side table.

(ABOVE)

Downlighting is what this setting is all about - a spotlight highlights the picture on the back wall, and another flatteringly lights the dining table.

Ratings:
Ambient: 4
Accent: 5
Task: 5
Decorative: 3
Kinetic: 1

Careful attention should be given to other objects in the room when creating a specific atmosphere. The dark wood table has not been covered, because it doesn't reflect light back up, so it helps to keep the room moody and romantic. The flowers, on the other hand, have been delicately lit by a small spotlight in the ceiling.

The lights in the pyramid cabinets offer a discreet means of preventing the room from becoming too dark. Turned down low, their light gently refracts in the glasses.

DINNER PARTY

Entertaining should be a theatrical occasion, with dramatic lighting to match. Following this line of thought, the room above has been downlit, with only areas of interest highlighted.

Isolating pictures and objects with strong contrasts of light and shade produces dramatic effects. Here, the candles and a spotlight frame the picture with a glowing arch of light. The halogen lights in the two pyramid cabinets are turned up slightly, transform-

ing the glasses into radiant, coloured lamps.

The table is at the heart of the room and is highlighted by a halogen spotlight, whose wide angle beam uses the white tablecloth as a large reflector. It bounces light up to flatteringly illuminate the faces of dinner guests and draw them together.

FAMILY TEA

When the dining room is to be used for reading, having tea or playing with the children, the lighting should be bright and functional, but still attractive as in the picture, above right. This is the bonus of having dimmer switches and lights spread evenly across the room.

The ceiling lights are on full and the middle one is focused on the table, so the newspaper is easy to read. The room is brightened further by lights in the pyramid cabinets and the picture light, which pinpoints the framed prints. Other decorative lights in the room add interest and help avoid any chance of blandness.

(ABOVE) *When using the dining room for more practical activities, it is best to be able to turn the lights up full, but add decorative lights to avoid blandness.*

Ratings:
Ambient: 5
Accent: 2
Task: 5
Decorative: 1
Kinetic: 0

(TOP) *Wall light*

(ABOVE) *Leax control switch*

(ABOVE) *Lit glasses*

Details and Tricks

WALL LIGHT

It is worth remembering how lighting can be shaded or coloured to complement wall colourings and textures. The parchment shades of this second-hand wall sconce perfectly match the tobacco colour of the walls. The light, which is a yellowy-brown, seeps out partly through the translucent shade and the top, but most of the light spill comes from the bottom of the shades. Because the lamp is mounted slightly off the wall, it casts its own shadows.

LIT GLASSES

The lights in the pyramid stands (above right) downlight three glass shelves and the glassware in them. The glasses refract the light and become lenses, giving the eerie impression that each glass is lit by a separate light.

LEAX CONTROL SWITCH

The Leax Control system is the last word in perfect control over a complete lighting system. It is easy to programme, and you can set the lights to give four combinations, all of which can be dimmed. However, careful planning of your lighting and the use of dimmer switches can give the same effect for less money.

DOWNLIGHTING AND UPLIGHTING

A striking way to illuminate an object is to downlight and uplight it. The vase-full of marbles to the right is lit from below by a sealed, waterproof halogen bulb recessed in the shelving. It is also lit from above making the patterns and texture of the flowers very clear and dramatic.

FRAMING PROJECTOR

A framing projector (below right) is perfect for highlighting any shape of picture, sculpture or ornament. Mounted in the ceiling, the metal cowl opens on one side and has a series of lenses behind it that gives the required shape for framing: it can be a soft-or hard-edged light. When lit by the framing projector, the pictures on the opposite wall in the dining room come to life.

CHECKLIST

* Lighting for dining must include kinetic, decorative and task lighting.

* Candles and chandeliers create a friendly and intimate atmosphere and can easily be backed up by other lighting such as recessed spotlights and one or two table lamps.

* Remember to light sideboards or tables from which food will be served.

(BELOW) *Downlighting and uplighting*

(BELOW) *Framing projector*

(BOTTOM) *Pictures lit by framing projector*

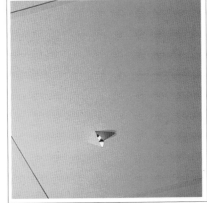

62

Even if your dining room is modern and minimal, use lighting imaginatively to capitalize on its main features. The basic ingredients of a modern room — white walls and the textures and colours of metal, glass and wood — respond well to a variety of lighting techniques. Although the rooms to the left and right have the same qualities, they have been used and lit quite differently.

Despite its contemporary design, the room to the left has religious overtones. The transparent glass table, raised on a platform, is reminiscent of the formality of a church altar. The lighting furthers this religious implication.

Accent lighting is provided by the recessed halogen bulbs in the wall-mounted unit, from which pools of very low light are emitted. Additionally, there is concealed lighting along the top and side of the unit, to create the illusion that the unit is moving away from the wall. This further enhances the ethereal quality of the room.

Wood, coupled with clever lighting is used to stop the room on the right from appearing cold and clinical. The glass wall, which could very easily look institutional, is transformed by the introduction of candlelight to the room. Above the table are several more candles, placed upon a glass shelf suspended from the ceiling – a modern interpretation of the traditional chandelier. This innovative light source is ideal, offering the advantages of a more usual chandelier in creating an intimate atmosphere for dining.

Planning the Light

The dining room, with its emphasis on entertaining, should be lit in a flattering and dramatic manner, controlled with dimmer switches. It is the ideal room in which to use chandeliers, candelabras and theatrical lampshades. For maximum flexibility, use a chandelier that can take either electric bulbs or candles. A mechanism for lowering the light over the dining table is also useful.

Because most dining rooms have a wooden table as their central feature, the chances are that this room will house a fair amount of dark wooden furniture. To counteract this, provide a cheerful light level or reflect existing light upwards by covering the table with a white tablecloth. To add a sense of theatre, accent-light pictures or collections of china with downlighters and up-lighters. Use the light to create a welcoming atmosphere to dine in.

(LEFT) *In this crisp dining room, natural light floods in from the skylight above the table, whose shape it echoes. The well also houses two small spotlights which emphasize the pictures behind the table.*

(RIGHT) *As well as being extremely decorative at night reflecting in the glass around the room, the kinetic light of the candles on the glass wall brings warmth to the room.*

APPROPRIATE FITTINGS

Lighting, for any room, should be chosen not only on the basis of the illumination required but also for how it complements the room and any other lighting in it. The room above, for example, appears to be lit solely by candles. In fact, the lighting is helped along by two unobtrusive lamps on the side table, their lights sympathetically adjusted to match the strength of the candles and their dark, opaque shades. These lamps give the room accent and ambient lighting without detracting from the striking, decorative light of the candles.

If you are going to use a chandelier over the dining table, it need not necessarily be a traditional one. Chandeliers can be made up of many things, like the one made from candles and shells (opposite, top left). It both flatters the room and is a witty object in its own right, suitably theatrical as a centrepiece. It is worth remembering that a chandelier need only support its own weight and so may be constructed of the flimsiest of materials. Often a simple piece of lighting like this can make all the difference in a room.

Lighting does not have to reflect exactly the style of the dining room, Here (top right), this style of lighting

(OPPOSITE, ABOVE AND RIGHT) *Intimacy can be created by subtle lighting such as that offered by the two very different chandeliers (opposite and above); lights hung so low that the light bounces back off the table (right), or by keeping the lights at the edges of the room (right, below).*

would be far too industrial and cold used on its own in a dining room setting. However, it is how it has been used that makes it an appropriate light source. In the first place, the lights have been hung very low to give the room a contemporary feel. Secondly and more importantly, by being this low, the light bounces back up off the table and on to the faces of the dinner guests. This produces the same effect as candles, drawing people together and creating a feeling of intimacy.

Lighting should always try to complement the architecture of a room, either by being incorporated into the design of the room or by illuminating its particular features. The major features in the room to the right are the wooden beams across the ceiling, which have been used to help light the room. The ceiling is uplit by a wooden lighting trough around the room, which gives off ambient light, while additional downlight sources are placed underneath the wall units. The wood and lighting work together well in this room, creating a warm and comfortable atmosphere.

Chapter 5

THE
BEDROOM

Increased luminous intensity is not what we are aiming for.
This is much too strong nowadays as it is, and we can no
longer endure it. Subdued lighting is the only
worthwhile objective.

PAUL SCHEERBART,
GLASS ARCHITECTURE
(1914)

The main source of light in a bedroom should
be ambient, in order to provide a neutral,
relaxing background. Other types of lighting
can be added, if needed, in the form of accent,
decorative and task lighting. These additions
should take into account the practical lighting
required for clothes, storage space and bedside
reading. It is useful to use directional light fittings on either side of the bed, overhead dimmable lights and low-voltage halogen spotlights for transforming the mood of the bedroom late at night.

(LEFT)
Candlelight always creates a most intimate atmosphere.

French Elegance

SETTING THE MOOD

(BELOW) *Overhead and bedside lamps, all with dimmer switches, make for a versatile lighting scheme.*

Bedrooms should have the ability to be both romantic and functional. They often need to be used as dormitory and dressing room as well as a place in which to relax and watch television, so a versatile and workable bedroom lighting scheme should include several different light sources that work in combination.

Here, perhaps more than in any other room of the house, the lighting levels will be adjusted throughout the evening and night, according to need,

Ratings:
Ambient: 4
Accent: 2
Task: 4
Decorative: 2
Kinetic: 0

(ABOVE)

Candlelight flatters skin tone much more than the harsh glare of tungsten or daylight and is therefore a soft, romantic light. Here, the level of background light is reduced and the chandelier is dimmed to a decorative twinkle. This encourages the candlelight to flourish without plunging the room into a murky gloom.

Ratings:
Ambient: 3
Accent: 0
Task: 0
Decorative: 0
Kinetic: 4

mood and the time of the year, so fit a dimmer switch to each lighting circuit that is installed. The French bedroom shown to the left displays a classic combination of traditional lighting sources; an overhead chandelier (*electrolier*) fitted with clear glass bulbs which twinkle on a low setting, and table lamps on either side of the bed. The lamps are fitted with thick, opaque shades that reduce glare to ease tired eyes.

ROMANTIC CANDLES

The two main light sources in the room above left – the chandelier and a concealed overhead uplighter – are enhanced and punctuated by natural candlelight. Dimmers are used for the chandelier and for the general ambient light given off by the hidden uplighter. This extra light, the one which we don't notice, gives the essential 'fill' to the room, offering warmth and security. It is placed inside the corona above the bed in a protective housing. This uplights the ceiling, but also manages to cast a little downlight through the

muslin of the corona – a delicate touch.

The overall lighting scheme is further embellished with candles for a more romantic feel. A candle's flame is more than romantic, it is seductive, and nowhere more so than in a subtly lit bedroom. Even today candlelight, in certain situations, offers a real alternative to electric lamps and does away with the need for plugs, wires and 'chased' walls.

The character of candlelight can be used to great effect anywhere – in chandeliers or wall sconces, in intimate or grand settings. Curiously, the romantic effect of candles is greater when they are used not alone, but as supplementary details against an ambient light set at a very low level.

A BOOK AT BEDTIME

An entirely different soft and ethereal mood can be established by light cast from a hidden uplighter, such as that in the room above right. Set at full power, it bounces light off the ceiling and produces a relaxed atmosphere.

(ABOVE)

A classic combination of chandelier and table lamps is enhanced by recessed lighting above the corona.

Ratings:
Ambient: 5
Accent: 0
Task: 4
Decorative: 0
Kinetic: 0

(ABOVE) *Candles*

Details and Tricks

CANDLES

This French bedroom displays a decorative style based on later 18th- and early 19th-century French traditions. Candlelight was the only source of light in such interiors, so the choice of candlelight here is an obvious one, for both romantic and historical reasons.

The domination of candles as a sole light source was challenged as early as the 1700s, when the Argand lamp (named after its inventor) appeared in domestic bourgeois homes. A sooty, but bright and very fashionable oil lamp, it revolutionized the way ordinary people spent their evenings, liberating them from the routine of always going to bed with the sun.

Today our choice of lighting styles has been vastly increased and is ever expanding, but it is still important to try and make room for the humble candle. It offers a quality of light that electricity cannot match; a yellow warmth, softness, no glare, and the charm of constantly moving light.

In the photograph above left candlelight is reflected in a clever combination of glass and mirror in this charming silhouette frame. Fabrics such as linen and silk, used here as a hanger, sparkle magically when set behind a moving light, and the cut crystal mount refracts the light and appears to move as the flame dances in front of it.

(ABOVE) *Girandole*

GIRANDOLE

The qualities of candlepower can be exploited even more subtly by introducing other highly reflective materials behind a candle, such as glass, ceramics or mirror. A popular 18th-century trick was to install a mirror behind a wall sconce, to form a girandole, such as that illustrated above right. This reflected the light into the room and tricked the eye into believing that double the number of candles were being used. The same effect can also be created by positioning a glazed picture or a pale-coloured glazed plate behind a flame, or the effect can be further enhanced by placing other large mirrors around the room.

TABLE LAMP

By fitting a shade so opaque that it hardly glows, but instead throws the light upwards and downwards, you create the perfect bedtime reading light (see below left). If you prefer a hard light, use a clear tungsten bulb. A pearl finish bulb will diffuse the light from the small light source that is the filament, and so casts a much softer shadow. The height of the lamp base and the size of the shade are also critical in a bedside lamp; the bulb must arrive at a point high enough to downlight onto a book, but must be shaded quite steeply so as not to shine on too much of the pillow.

To create a similar colour light to that of a candle, use the kind of soft yellow effect bulb that all electrical stores now sell. Sadly, it is impossible to produce this warm, gentle light with tungsten bulbs, which give a full spectrum of pure white light, or with compact fluorescents, which tend to project either a pink or bluish-green cast, even when shaded.

CORONA

A decorative or architectural device such as the ornate corona featured below right provides perfect cover for a discreet uplighter. Coronas, four-posters or half-tester beds have the added advantage of fabric hangings which can hide a power cable, contained in a conduit and fixed flush to the wall. Hidden light establishes a general level of soft light most successfully. Preferably it should be on the ceiling, where no candle is going to have to compete for attention.

CHECKLIST

* Dimmable ceiling uplighters with ordinary tungsten bulbs.

* Side table lamps with mains voltage fittings and opaque shades.

* Table or wall lamps with moveable 'swan neck' armatures for positioning the reading lights.

* Fibre-optic reading lamps for providing a very small lit area.

* Decorative chandelier to contemplate when in bed, fitted with either low voltage dimmable lamps or mains voltage tungsten clear lamps.

(BELOW) *Table lamp*

(BELOW) *Corona*

Planning the Light

When lighting any room by daylight, it is useful to remember that a north-facing window creates ambient light from a reflective northern sky, while a south-facing one can provide accent light from strong direct sunlight.

In certain circumstances, such as in hot climates, lighting has to help create a cool ambience. This has been successfully accomplished in the room to the left. The solution for this house has been to place the lighting far away from the bed, either by concealing it behind the walls or, as in the case of the two reflector spotlights, high above the bed. Although the major source of light is ambient, with the white walls and ceiling reflecting the light around the room, the two spotlights can double up as task lighting. In short, the lighting scheme helps to psychologically cool down the room.

It is important to remember, however, that in a bedroom, direct sunlight can be quite overpowering and distracting. The simplest and best solution is to use see-through nets or, as in the case bottom left, two layers of muslin over the window. Filtering sunlight through fabric is like placing a diffusing shade over a lamp — it makes for a much softer, low-level ambient light, giving the room a calm, romantic atmosphere, even during the day.

Artificial and natural sources can work together, as seen opposite, top. Here, two halogen lamps are dimmed to a warmer tone and used to uplight the ceiling, providing a yellower contrast to the rather bluish natural light coming through the window. The halogens soften the somewhat stark contours and colours of the room. A

(ABOVE LEFT AND LEFT) *Two very different ways of lighting a room in a hot climate. Keep the room cool by either placing the lighting far away from the bed, or filter direct sunlight through fabric to create a soft ambient light.*

(ABOVE AND LEFT) *The effect created by halogen uplights during the day is quite different to that at night-time.*

cheaper alternative would be to use ordinary warm, tungsten lighting.

At night (left) the same lamps are turned up full, uplighting the ceiling with a much whiter light than available daylight. The room is cast in a grey ambient light which is still very warm and relaxing.

(ABOVE) *The table and ceiling lamps in this bedroom have been used to subdue the strongly contrasting ceiling and wall colours by only lighting very local areas. Because the room looks darker at night, its character is not overpowered by the qualities of either colour.*

LIGHT AND COLOUR

If you want to use strong colours in your bedroom but do not want them to dominate, use two complementary colours. In the bedroom above, the colours red and green have been used, which are perhaps too powerful on their own, but together they cancel out each other's potency. The lighting should be decorative or accent and not ambient, as is usual in a bedroom. This helps to reduce the powerful effect of the colours as bedtime approaches.

ADDITIONAL AMBIENT LIGHT SOURCES

The ambient light in a bedroom need not come from the usual sources. For example, in the room above, it comes, in part, from the recessed spotlights in the ceiling. More interestingly, it is generated too from the spotlight arrangement also used for task lighting. The spotlights provide ambient light by downlighting the floor, which bounces the light back up to illuminate part of the room.

(ABOVE) *Throwing light onto the floor can be a very useful way of creating ambient light in a bedroom, as lighting from above can prove distracting when lying on the bed.*

Chapter 6

THE BATHROOM

In the entire art of lighting, the moment of
fascinosum is stronger than
the tremendum.

HANS SEDLMAYR,
LIGHT IN ITS ARTIFICIAL MANIFESTATIONS
(1978)

The bathroom is often neglected when it comes to lighting. However, with a careful approach the room can be transformed from a place of fast ablutions and sanitaryware into an exotic, inviting room, a place to spend time relaxing.

As this bathroom shows, all that is needed is a simple combination of three elements: an imaginative use of functional lighting, the introduction of special lighting when needed and the occasional, ingenious use of objects commonly found in bathrooms – mirrors, bottles, glass and water.

(LEFT) *The best way to create a calm, relaxed atmosphere in the bathroom is by using candles.*

A Luxury Soak

ROMAN BATH

This lighting has been designed to make the most of the bathroom's sybaritic connotations. Full use has been made of the bath itself, the surrounding marble and the glass and mirror arches.

The functional ceiling halogen spotlights lend task and accent lighting. The bath has been isolated by one solitary light, making it the central feature of the room, its stark whiteness a symbol of clarity and purity.

Another spotlight has been focused on the shelves where coloured bottles provide a dramatic decorative feature. The shell on the top shelf has been specifically highlighted. Lighting objects such as shells, or lotions and potions, means that they are reflected and refracted in the mirrors, the glass and the bath water. The overall cast of light gives this bathroom a calm aura

Ratings:
Ambient: 4
Accent: 4
Task: 5
Decorative: 1
Kinetic: 2

(BELOW) *Coloured bottles and a shell have been carefully lit to add decorative details to this bathroom.*

(ABOVE)
Underwater lighting creates really attractive patterns in the bath water which arrest the eye.

Ratings:
Ambient: 5
Accent: 0
Task: 0
Decorative: 0
Kinetic: 0

and an instant lift, adding colour and creating a distraction from the bathroom's more mundane uses.

At night, if there were no frosted glass, the windows would become black mirrors. Instead, a coloured light installed outside creates a wonderfully atmospheric glow.

TURKISH BATHS

With just a subtle change in lighting, the atmosphere has been transformed from that of a tranquil Roman spa to a steamy, exotic Turkish bath. The room featured above left now feels warm and relaxing; ideal for a jacuzzi, a massage and for shedding the stresses and strains of the day.

All that has happened is that the ceiling lights have been turned off and instead, the room has been uplit by a sealed-unit uplighter mounted on the wall. With its dimmer switch and frosted glass filter to diffuse the light, the lamp offers a number of different levels of ambient lighting to suit the different requirements of a bathroom.

A waterproof light mounted inside the bath contributes to the uplighting of the room and draws attention to the moving patterns in the bath, help-

ing to give the room its restful atmosphere.

ROMANTIC

Candles will completely metamorphose the bathroom. The room will instantly become a meditative place, perfectly lit for a romantic bath for two.

Here (above right), only three candelabras, each fitted with three candles, are used to light the bathroom. They are repeated almost *ad infinitum* in the mirrors, the glass and even the ceramic surface of the bath.

The shell is lit from behind with a special sealed-unit, 12-volt lamp for the bathroom. It is a unique feature and a source of warm, sultry light. The coloured bottles standing around the bath — which sparkle and reflect the candlelight — complete the romantic effect.

Always check with your electrician that what you are specifying conforms to national regulations for bathroom fittings (see page 134). It is essential that the lighting unit is sealed and moisture-proof and that the light source cannot be directly accessed by hand.

(ABOVE) *Extra light and decoration for this romantic setting are provided by the floating candles in the bath.*

Ratings:
Ambient: 0
Accent: 0
Task: 0
Decorative: 5
Kinetic: 5

Details and Tricks

SHELL LAMPSHADE

A light hidden behind a shell (above) is both unusual and subtle. The shell's patterns and grains glow warmly and the light is also cast onto the bottles below through the glass shelves.

CHANDELIER

This chandelier (opposite, top left) is a good example of a lamp being used for more than just providing light. The glass bottom is filled with water which is then moved around by a paddle. It is soothing and hypnotic. The transformer for this and the bulb is hidden in the ceiling.

ALCOVE

Any boring corner can be given an uplift by light. The otherwise uninter-esting drinking tap in an alcove (opposite, bottom left) has been downlit by a halogen spotlight. The light is functional and helps to make the area more attractive.

SINK LIGHTS

When it comes to the everyday bathroom chores such as shaving, putting on make-up or cleaning teeth, good task lighting is essential.

Here (opposite, top right), two tungsten spotlights are installed above the sink, each three-quarters of the way around the top of the mirror. Shadows from each source are cancelled out by the light from the other. In this way, the face is both evenly and flatteringly lit. The light is still suitably bright but not glaring, as it would be if a light had been placed directly above.

MAKE-OVER

As with the lights over the sink, lighting the face requires an even, shadowless cast. One solution is to use five pearl 40-watt (or 25-watt) golf bulbs down each side of a mirror as below, bottom right. The smaller the light source, the stronger the shadows, so by using pearl bulbs, the light can be diffused.

CHECKLIST

* Make the most of objects commonly found in bathrooms, such as glass, water and mirrors, lighting them to good effect.

* Ensure that areas used for shaving and applying make-up are well and clearly lit.

(BELOW)
Chandelier

(LEFT) *Sink lights*

(BELOW)
Make-over

(RIGHT) *Alcove*

(ABOVE) *The diffused light given off by the bulbs surrounding the mirror is perfect for lighting the face.*

Planning the Light

When planning bathroom lighting, it is essential to provide the right level of task and ambient lighting and to work out a way of blending the lighting into the room. The two bathrooms featured above and opposite, one contemporary and one period, illustrate how you can resolve the balance between ambient and task lighting and incorporate them into the overall design of the room.

For functional lighting around the sink, one of the most successful options is the theatrical make-up mirror, which lights the face in a flattering manner from all angles. It is a piece of pure task lighting, comprising numerous 25-watt frosted golf bulbs which surround the mirror on three sides. The bulbs in the bathroom above are placed far enough away from the centre of the mirror and are of a sufficiently low wattage not to glare or interfere with any reflected image.

In this bathroom, the lighting

trough above the sink provides the room with its ambient light. It uplights the ceiling and provides downlights, using recessed halogen spotlights which, like the golf bulbs, produce a play of reflected light in the surrounding metal surfaces. Do, however, consult an electrician about placing light sources near water.

Using a lighting trough or a false ceiling to conceal lights means you can avoid disturbing plasterwork to rechannel a room for a new lighting scheme.

Whatever the design of your bathroom, try to create the optimum amount of task and ambient lighting. The bathroom above, although different in feel and arrangement from the one opposite still has a similar lighting level. If you have a traditional bathroom in a period house, this room demonstrates how to achieve the right level of ambient light without sacrificing the period setting.

Uplighting is provided by a wall-mounted lamp which sits easily in the

(ABOVE) *Traditional decoration can best be lit by uplighters, either mounted on the wall or in a central bowl.*

decorative scheme, as does the bathroom's main light source, an alabaster bowl hung from the ceiling. This shade (it could equally be of etched or frosted glass) filters much of the light, providing a low level of task and decorative light and a high level of ambient light. When the lamp is dimmed, as here, it provides a glowing, relaxing light as a background for a long, indulgent bath. When turned up full, the lamp provides enough task light for the numerous other functions of the bathroom. The mirrors help to reflect and refract this main source of light around the room.

A bathroom, like a kitchen, requires both task and ambient lighting. In some cases, decorative fittings can provide both types of lighting. Particular attention should be paid to the task lighting above and around the sink. Apart from providing functional light, the scheme should be versatile enough to create a relaxing scheme when having a bath.

Task lighting comes from several sources in the picture featured to the left: some comes from a lamp in the skylight, some from the lighting trough above the sink, and a trace from the concealed lights behind the mirrors. Although this lighting system is very clever, it is not completely satisfactory, since the overall lighting level is high on ambient but low on task – good for the room's character but not so good for shaving by.

DAYLIGHT
When planning your lighting scheme, you should take into consideration the amount of daylight your bathroom receives. Natural light can be used in exciting ways to provide much of the bathroom's ambient and task lighting. However, as the examples opposite and overleaf show, much depends on the bathroom's design. The bathroom to the right, built mostly of glass, has no need for internal lighting. During the

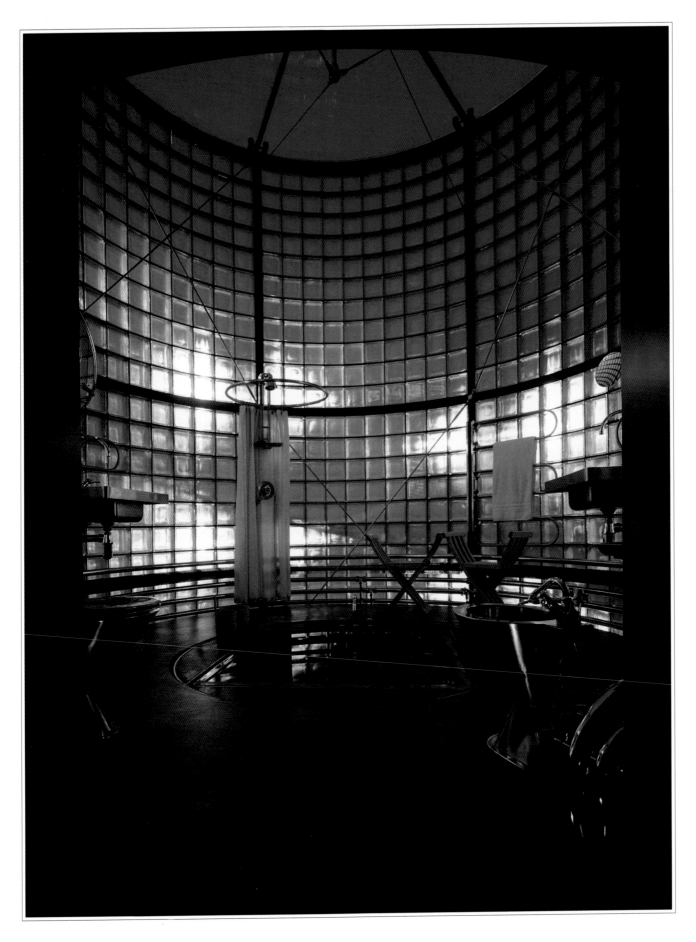

(ABOVE) *This arrangement makes maximum use of daylight as a source of task light – to illuminate the user's reflection.*

day it is ablaze with sunlight streaming in through the glass roof and walls. At night, it is beautifully lit by moonlight and by the arrangement of artificial lights placed outside the building to supplant the sun.

Many bathrooms would not have the grandeur of the one above left, but even quite ordinary windows can be used to great effect. The common criticism of this room might be that it is 'over-designed', but the use of high

(ABOVE) *For daylight to be truly successful as an ambient form of lighting it is neccessary to have large windows, or several smaller ones.*

windows as light-sources to illuminate one's face in the mirrors below is a very novel feature. However, it is important not to place cleverness over functionalism. For example, here there is little ambient light despite the three classically arranged, wall-mounted sconces. By day, the uncovered half of the window allows daylight in, but even this does not provide enough ambient light to light this bathroom successfully.

A hot, sunny climate offers an opportunity to use natural light in much more exciting ways, as shown above right. Three small windows have been placed at the top of the room, just below the eaves of the roof to catch the daylight reflected off the ground up onto the eaves. As a result, there is little directional light in the room. Instead, we find a cool, general level of ambient light. Meanwhile, by contrast, the lower window acts as a direct and functional light source.

Chapter 7

THE STUDY

It is a rule of thumb that enough scattered light should be emitted from the ceiling and the illuminated walls for all parts of the room to be clearly visible. In addition, all important spots in the room — such as a desk, a piano, or the page of a book — may also be illuminated using specially directed light...Powerful spot lighting enhances the cosy aspect of a living room or library.

W.C. POSEY, HYGIENE OF THE EYE
(1918)

For those who have ever worked in an office, poor lighting and the associated problems of eye strain, can often only worsen an already hostile environment. The home office or study, however, offers us the opportunity to provide good work lighting, with glaring fluorescent tubes banned once and for all in favour of the versatile and practical halogen light.

Halogen bulbs, whether providing background lighting or task lighting, give the nearest illumination to natural daylight.

This is the best artificial light for reading, writing or working on a computer, since it gives a strong, concentrated beam of light with little glare or spill.

Although there are now daylight-equivalent fluorescent tubes, which are useful for workshops, most have a green or pink colour value and, unlike halogen lamps, fluorescent tubes cannot be dimmed.

(LEFT)

The study shown here demonstrates ways of keeping the lighting level at the same intensity throughout the day.

Concentrated Effort

DAYTIME AND WORKTIME

Daylight can cause frustrating problems when working on a computer: it can turn the screen into a mirror, reflecting the room and any natural light from a window, creating a bright, glaring distraction. However, cutting out all the daylight is an unsatisfactory solution, as there is nothing more depressing than working in a darkened room with only artificial light to guide your eyes during the day.

In the study below, the glare and the reflection on the computer have been minimized by turning the computer slightly away from the window, which in turn has been half covered by a blackout blind. This type of blind is much more useful than another type of blind such as a Venetian one, which offers only a partial block. This one blacks out most of the window but allows plenty of natural daylight to pour in onto the table adjacent to the computer. Another advantage is that the eyes can rest on the unfixed horizon outside the window – a necessary relaxation exercise for computer users.

A multi-purpose halogen lamp further enhances the daylight by uplighting the ceiling so that it acts as a giant reflector. This type of halogen light with its own dimmer switch caters for most office needs (see Details, page 92).

Ratings:
Ambient: 5
Accent: 0
Task: 5
Decorative: 0
Kinetic: 0

(BELOW) *This is the ideally lit study for working during the day; the window is half covered to reduce glare and the ceiling reflects the light from the halogen lamp to enhance the daylight.*

(ABOVE) *Once it is dark, extra light needs to be provided. Two spotlights have now been switched on.*

Ratings:
Ambient: 5
Accent: 2
Task: 1
Decorative: 0
Kinetic: 0

When working during the day, the overall light should be restful on the eyes; it should be of a high ambient level with no visible sources and, therefore, no glare — identical, in fact, to the light level required for watching television.

The eyes need to have an area to fix on, too, and this can be provided by accent or task lighting which, as in this case, can be placed next to the computer.

NIGHT-TIME

When working in the office at night, lighting should be kept at a level that is similar to daytime light. Contrast between shade and light can be eliminated almost entirely by a high level of ambient light.

The halogen lamp in the photograph above left, uplights the ceiling in an even glow, which is reflected around the room. In this way, the ceiling has become a gigantic lamp. There are no shadows, as there would be if the room was downlit by a central source of light.

Extra light comes from the downlighting behind the computer provid-ed by two directional spotlights clipped onto the bookshelves. Again, with this kind of lighting, glare or reflection on the computer is kept to a minimum.

AFTER HOURS

Working late at night can be a much more pleasurable experience if you have paid careful attention to the lighting. Without losing functional light, the study can be lit to look warm and relaxing.

Three sources of ambient lighting help to create the atmosphere in the office illustrated in the photograph above. The directional spotlights have been hidden from view on lower shelves. They provide an attractive uplight for the books, while also light-ing the ceiling, to give a shadowless, non-glaring light source.

A table lamp is used to create a very soft background light. The pearl bulb diffuses the light, as does the translucent egg-shaped shade.

On the opposite wall to the desk there is a decorative wall light which softly uplights another part of the ceiling.

(ABOVE) *When the work is over and it is time for a more relaxed atmosphere, turn the halogen uplight into a down-light and focus its beam onto part of the desk - now that the computer is turned off, you will need this light to read by.*

Ratings:
Ambient: 3
Accent: 3
Task: 5
Decorative: 2
Kinetic: 0

(ABOVE)
Halogen lamp

Details and Tricks

HALOGEN LAMP

A multi-purpose, mains-voltage halogen lamp can give a number of different effects. It can take a 150-, 300- or 500-watt bulb, according to the size of the room, and can wash a white wall with a very warm light produced at a low setting. The one above is adjustable to any height within the range of its 1.75m (8 ft) stand and the maximum throw of light onto the ceiling is when the lamp is positioned just above eye level. A halogen lamp such as this can uplight or downlight and the clear white light can be dimmed or diffused to suit any purpose.

WALL LIGHT

By comparison, a wall uplighter fitted with a soft reflector bulb will cast glare-free ambient light onto a ceiling. If a light is too high on a wall, the light cast from it will be too localized.

The lower the light, the greater the area of ceiling that is lit and therefore, a better ambient effect is achieved.

REFLECTOR LIGHT

The spotlight below left is a reflector lamp with a small E14 Edison screw bulb. The clips and turning mechanism makes it directional and versatile; it can be used to light any part of the room. Like the halogen lamp, it can be multi-purpose, providing background or task lighting.

EGG LAMP

The egg-shaped table lamp below right lends the office a warm atmosphere. For a diffused glowing light, use a lamp that incorporates a large shade, like this 'egg'.

CHECKLIST

* A study needs both task and ambient lighting. In both cases, the light source should be non-glare and shielded from the eyes.

* The most suitable lamps are halogen, they are very versatile and provide the best type of light when reading, writing and working on the computer.

* Ensure that light is spread as wide as possible but using a diffuse lamp.

(BELOW)
Reflector light

(BELOW)
Egg lamp

(ABOVE AND RIGHT) *Whether you are lighting a whole room or part of a room, the lights need to be multi-functional for a work area. Concentrate on finding a light that blends in well with its environment.*

Planning the Light

A study or workspace requires non-glare task and ambient lighting. The simplest way to create the right lighting is to use a multi-functional lamp, preferably halogen, for its whiteness. You need to be able to move the lamp around, above and below eye level.

INTEGRATED LIGHTING

The light above left demonstrates that you do not have to forego versatility and style, even in a functional workspace. This industrial aluminium spun lamp is fully integrated into the high-tech aesthetics of the room. So much so, it looks like it is an integral part of the shelf fittings. It has a flexible tube

arm which allows it to move; it can rotate to produce task or accent lighting and can even produce ambient lighting when turned to illuminate the ceiling.

A flexible principle has been employed above right for a workspace which is part of a much larger room. The French industrial work lamps are exactly what the workspace needs, yet their design also complements the rest of the room. They are like low-slung Anglepoise lights and are as versatile. The lamps produce non-glare task lighting, are pulled down to below eye-level, and also supply accent lighting for objects on the desk, or ambient lighting when reflected off the wall.

Chapter 8

THE GARDEN

Artificial light finds its origins amidst nocturnal sorcery, mysteries, celebrations and feasts. The animal paintings of the palaeolithic caves were created by torchlight; they were also seen by the initiated in the light of the torches that brought them to life.

HANS SEDLMAYR, LIGHT IN ITS ARTIFICIAL
MANIFESTATIONS (1978)

There are a number of key elements for lighting a garden successfully that are simple but not random. Nothing magical will happen by placing a couple of lamps in the bushes or floodlighting the garden like a football stadium.

Some of the best results can be had from lighting specific plants and structures – throwing silhouetted light onto a wall – or backlighting plants and flowers.

An enchanting garden can be created by the clever use of garden ornaments and architecture, brown and green foliage, mirrors and water. It also helps to have a central focus, like the tree in the garden featured overleaf.

Garden lighting is available nowadays from a wide variety of sources and includes specialist architectural uplighting, exterior floodlights, spotlights, lamps and candles.

(LEFT)

Backlighting foliage creates an almost fluorescent effect.

Evening Greenery

PARTY FLARE

You don't need a national festival such as 4 July or 5 November as an excuse to add flare to your garden. Naked flames perfectly complement nature, while adding an extra-special ingredient to parties. In the photograph below, the candle flares lead towards the back of the garden, as if in a torch-light procession. They are sheathed in a muslin wick rather than a conventional one, so as not to blow out in the wind.

The curved mirror on the back wall bounces light from the flares back onto the garden. The result is a powerful and stimulating setting, emphasized by the glowing leaves of the tree,

(BELOW)
Flares create an enthusiastic welcome to any garden party. They are easy to position, too.

Ratings:
Ambient: 0
Accent: 2
Task: 0
Decorative: 5
Kinetic: 5

(ABOVE) *A tree is simple to light - it just requires a single, powerful, uplighter - and it instantly becomes the focal point of the garden.*

Ratings:
Ambient: 0
Accent: 4
Task: 0
Decorative: 5
Kinetic: 0

which is lit by a buried uplighter hidden at its base.

If it is not practical to party by candlelight alone, extra lighting can be provided by an ordinary electrical outdoor light placed at the back of the garden.

THE MAGIC TREE

The easiest way to vary the garden's image is by installing lights on different circuits which are controlled by dimmer switches. The lighting used above left gives an effect which is reminiscent of childhood fairytales. The light at the base of the tree has been turned up to be as bright as possible, as has the uplighting behind the foliage in the raised flowerbed at the back of the garden.

The leaves on the tree glitter like silver and the garden becomes a magical, mystical secret garden. A mirror confuses the eye with a trompe l'oeil effect of depth and adds to the fairytale impression, as do the shadows cast from the conservatory lights at

the front of the garden and the solitary downlighting of a plant from a lamp on a stalk.

BLUE MOON

Enhancing the products of mother nature is one of the major pleasures of garden lighting. Very rarely, except in movies, are gardens bathed naturally in the blue light of the moon. However, by installing two PAR 38 floodlamps with blue lenses at the front of the garden, this garden has had its own romantic moonlight installed artificially. (The other two colour lenses suitable for the garden are green and yellow but, unlike blue, they can give a sickly hue.)

Lighting on the two separate circuits is turned down low, so that the soft blue light gently picks out the main features in the garden. The other lighting around the garden – in the raised flowerbeds, on the lawn and on the bed nearest the conservatory – produces interesting splotches of complementary yellow light.

(ABOVE) *For more subtle lighting, use floodlamps with blue lenses warmed by individual pools of yellow light.*

Ratings:
Ambient: 4
Accent: 5
Task: 0
Decorative: 5
Kinetic: 0

(ABOVE) *Spotlight*

Details and Tricks

SPOTLIGHT
The highlighting of this rosemary plant (above left) shows the stunning effect achieved by focusing light onto a solitary object. This is created simply by angling the spotlight in the tree. The tube (baffle) which is attached to the light reduces the spill of the beam. This throws a precise spotlight onto the plant, increasing the theatricality of the effect.

CANDLES
Candles, like flares, are great sources of kinetic light for special occasions. The citronella candles above right have attractive containers which add to the party atmosphere.

SPHERE
Lighting man-made objects, such as strong pieces of open and unpretentious architecture, add drama to a garden. Uplighting is thrown onto an open globe, opposite top left, where every spar radiates light. Because of

the globe's design you cannot see the source of light, which you would with a solid object.

(ABOVE) *Candles*

PLANT LIGHT
The lighting of a specific plant is immeasurably more dramatic than the provision of a general light source. It produces a strong and structured look, proving how light can successfully be used to emphasize and enhance single objects.

The plant (opposite, top right) is lit by a spiked garden uplighter mounted in the earth. The beam of light follows the plant as it winds and grows up the beanpoles and throws interesting shadows onto what would otherwise be a boring shed.

LEAVES
A simple but effective lighting trick is to backlight a plant from below, to make it look as though someone has literally 'switched on' the leaves. Here (opposite, bottom left), fallen leaves are backlit by a lamp buried in the ground. The effect is almost that of a stained-glass window.

URN

The halogen uplighter (below, bottom right) encased in a waterproof fitting, with a clasp for easy attachment, illustrates how lighting can be used to illuminate architecture. In this case the urn is lit from below to give a dramatic effect, while the plants in the urn provide an organic silhouette. The wonderful versatility of this light means that you can either place the source in a pot or you can bury it in the earth.

Lighting plants and garden architecture in this way is a fine way of bringing individuality to your garden.

CHECKLIST

* To transform a garden for different occasions, the lighting should be on different circuits, each with dimmer switches.

* Best types of garden lighting are decorative, kinetic and accent.

* Using coloured lenses on floodlamps can be extremely effective, whilst flares or candles are great for parties.

* Light architectural features or individual plants for special effect.

(RIGHT) *Sphere*

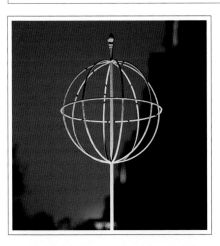

(LEFT) *Plant light*

(RIGHT) *Leaves*

(LEFT) *Urn*

(ABOVE) *An entire building can be viewed as a giant lamp sitting in a landscape.*

Planning the Light

It is important to remember that a house with large, or many, windows will have an impact on the landscape at night: therefore any lighting design should consider how it complements and blends in with the house's natural surroundings.

The house above looks warm and inviting because all the lights are switched on. Every room is aglow and the effect is built on by using candlelight at and around the dining table.

SIMPLE SCHEMES

The case study shown on pages 98 and 99 illustrates how lighting is best used in a garden when hidden among, and illuminating, foliage or background surfaces behind foliage: it is then fully integrated. At first glance, the garden

above shows a simpler, less theatrical scheme than those already covered. The foliage is mainly front-lit producing less-than dramatic effects, and an over-all level of general ambient light is achieved from lighting placed along the underside of the pergola. It is a basic and adequate scheme, but one which is unfortunately seriously flawed by being too functional.

The light source used is fluorescent strips which cannot be dimmed, and offer unsympathetic colours to foliage. They are positioned too high to be unobtrusive, offering instead uncomfortable levels of glare at night, and they serve to light nothing well but the pergola itself and the path running around the edge of the pond. Unless you are installing safety lighting by footpaths, try to avoid lighting the obvious and the mundane.

(ABOVE) *Successful garden lighting depends on working with plants*, not *paths.*

(ABOVE) *The Indian Sky Lantern festival along the banks of the river Varnasi shows the beauty of woven rush lanterns, hung on poles.*

LIGHT AND RITUAL

Garden lighting should be all about creating a magical environment, so consider it an opportunity to indulge your imagination. The power and the magic of light have deep ritualistic roots; in numerous ceremonies around the world, moving, living flames symbolize life's spirituality and man's soul.

When lighting your garden, whether for specific occasions or special parties, it is easy to copy and adapt from the world's many festivals. Lanterns, such as those featured above, look stunning hung around the garden and are cheap and easy to make. In the USA and Europe, Hallowe'en night celebrates the spirit world when the candle behind the

WATERY LIGHTS

pumpkin's features becomes the soul inside the face. It is the spirit dancing behind the eyes.

The Spanish on the other hand exploit a more dramatic use of naked flame in the fire dragon pageant in Barcelona. Using a live, bright white light which sheds falling sparks, an unearthly atmosphere is created by this most exciting use of natural light.

Any water feature in the garden, whether pond or swimming pool, deserves to be lit. The best way is from underneath using specially designed waterproof fittings. Movement of the water, from fountains, waterfalls or wind is the necessary addition to turn decorative light into kinetic light.

(ABOVE) *Although water movement can make patterns of light, this still reflection helps this house to assert itself in the landscape, adding a new geometry to its architecture.*

PRACTICALITIES

However perfect a lamp may be, it does not in itself represent

a complete lighting system. It is only part of a whole.

HENRY DE PARVILLE,
L'ELECTRICITE ET SES APPLICATIONS
(1883)

This section of the book begins by providing practical information on how to install or improve your own lighting scheme, starting with a visual reference aid to help you plan your lighting. The contents list opposite shows you exactly what is included in this glossary. The most important quality about any lamp or light fitting is not what it looks like, but how it performs. Consequently, the photographs of lights and lamps show you not only the fittings, but also the kind of light that they cast - necessary information to form a judgement.

It is, of course, impossible to cover every fitting and every historical period, so the items have been chosen because they represent a breed of fitting or a type of lighting.

The section then gives vital information on how to contact and choose electricians and how to plan your requirements. Full safety information is provided as well as detailed reference charts which show how light works.

Practicalities Contents

THE PHOTOGRAPHIC GLOSSARY

BULBS AND FITTINGS
(MAINS-VOLTAGE)

Although the choice of light bulbs on the market is vast, a representative sample showing the variety of different types and sizes is shown here, together with a selection of standard bulb holders.

1 Opal Candles
A more recent invention, the opal-finish bulb produces an even softer light than a pearl bulb, with only one per cent efficiency loss. It is achieved by means of coating the inside of the glass.

2 Mains-voltage Halogen
This type of bulb is also available in more conventional shapes. It operates by a clever molecular reaction that occurs between the halogen gas in the tube and the tungsten filament (hence tungsten-halogen), producing a very bright clear white light. See the chart on pages 136-39 for a full comparison.

3 Candle Bulbs
Candle bulbs come as 60 watts maximum. (The size of the glass 'envelope' prevents anything more powerful.)

4 Pygmy Bulbs (x 3)
Useful for making hidden lamps even more discreet.

5 Appliance Bulb
For specialist applications.

**6 Mains-voltage
Tungsten Tube**
Nearly every bulb on this page is of the ordinary tungsten type, which produces light from a glowing filament held in an inert gas. They are popular, cheap to produce and easily disposable. Although they pro-

duce a warm light that is flattering to skintones, they are generally limited in their application, providing a maximum of 150 watts of light.

7 Decorative Globe Bulb
Several manufacturers have attempted to make the bulb more attractive and safer in effect by enlarging the surface area that is coated.

8 GLS Bulbs
The earliest bulbs were blown from clear glass, but to reduce glare a frosted or pearl version was soon produced by etching the inside surface of the glass. This diffuses the light source inside the bulb, giving softer shadows.

9 Crown-silvered GLS Bulb
Useful for directional light and in lamps where glare is unwanted.

10 Chandelier Bulb
Other fittings are available, including the tiny E10 for decorative candle bulbs (see Electric Candles on page 126).

11 Golf Ball Bulb

12 ES Phenolic Fitting with Shade Ring
The following fittings are the most usual fittings for domestic mains-voltage lighting, made in some countries from black phenolic plastic and in

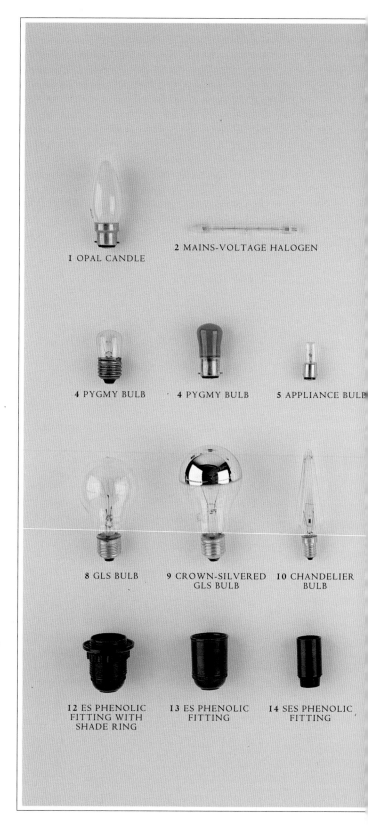

1 OPAL CANDLE   2 MAINS-VOLTAGE HALOGEN

4 PYGMY BULB   4 PYGMY BULB   5 APPLIANCE BULB

8 GLS BULB   9 CROWN-SILVERED GLS BULB   10 CHANDELIER BULB

12 ES PHENOLIC FITTING WITH SHADE RING   13 ES PHENOLIC FITTING   14 SES PHENOLIC FITTING

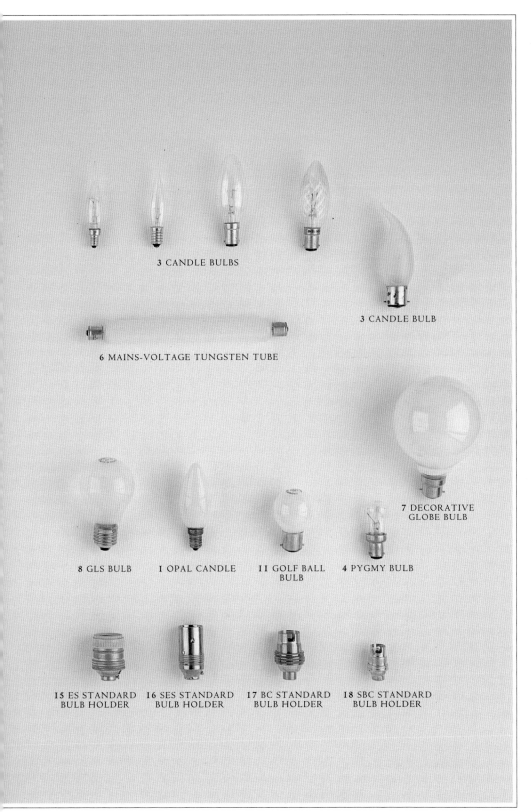

3 CANDLE BULBS

3 CANDLE BULB

6 MAINS-VOLTAGE TUNGSTEN TUBE

7 DECORATIVE
GLOBE BULB

8 GLS BULB   1 OPAL CANDLE   11 GOLF BALL
BULB   4 PYGMY BULB

15 ES STANDARD
BULB HOLDER   16 SES STANDARD
BULB HOLDER   17 BC STANDARD
BULB HOLDER   18 SBC STANDARD
BULB HOLDER

others from brass, sometimes with a ceramic insert as shown, for added safety insulation.

13 ES Phenolic Fitting

14 SES Phenolic Fitting

15 ES Standard Bulb Holder
The Edison Screw, also known as E27, is 27mm wide.

16 SES Standard Bulb Holder

17 BC Standard Bulb Holder
Bayonet cap, or B22

18 SBC Standard Bulb Holder
Small bayonet cap, or B15

110   BULBS: MORE EXOTIC SOURCES

*The conventional GLS tungsten bulb is popular, but inefficient, providing
150 watts of light at most. If you want more light from a tiny source, you
must turn to halogen sources; a mains-voltage tube like the one shown on
the previous page can be rated anything from 150 to 700 watts.*

**1 Low-voltage Halogen
Uplighter for the Garden**
An exciting modern development in garden lighting has
been the introduction of low-
voltage halogen lamps into
garden luminaires. All outdoor
fittings must, of course, be
waterproof.

**2 Low-voltage Halogen
Downlighter for Small Plants**
This sleek and unobtrusive
fitting is designed specifically
to highlight individual plants.

3 Low-voltage Capsules
These capsules are intended
for use with a 12-volt transformer. They use anything
from 15 to 50 watts and produce a much whiter light than
their tungsten counterparts.

4 Dichroic Reflectors
Halogen lights can be bought
at their most simple as tiny
bulbs, called capsules, which
throw light in every direction.
They are normally sold
mounted in a glass dichroic
reflector, designed to throw
the light forward while allowing the considerable heat produced to project backwards
through the glass.

**5 Housing for Ceiling-
mounted Downlighter**
In a ceiling, dichroic reflectors
should always be installed by a
qualified electrician into a
heat-resistant fitting. This

excellent example is manufactured by John Cullen Lighting.

**6 Small Crown-silvered
Reflector Bulb**
The top bulb is crown silvered
which reflects the light backwards, usually into a reflective
fitting or shade.

7 R16 Reflector
(30° half-flood)
This reflector is an ordinary
tungsten bulb that throws the
light forwards in a beam.

8 R25 Reflector
(23° spot)
Similar to 7, above, this is a
more powerful bulb with a
wider angle of throw.

9 PAR 38 Reflector
(16° spot or 30° flood)
A more sophisticated relative of
the reflector bulb is the PAR
lamp which is made of cast
glass and incorporates a lense
front, giving a choice of powerful spot or floodlight (see bulbs
chart on pages 140-1).

**10 Compact Fluorescent
for Table Lamps**
Although no larger than a GLS
bulb, the miniature fluorescent
produces the equivalent of a 40-
watt output, using only 9 watts.
The light produced is quite
harsh in colour but the bulbs
do not get very hot, so offer a
safe choice for garages, workshops or children's bedrooms.

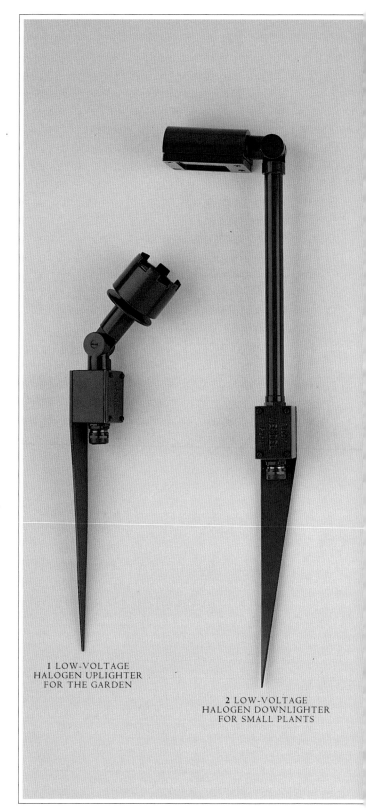

1 LOW-VOLTAGE
HALOGEN UPLIGHTER
FOR THE GARDEN

2 LOW-VOLTAGE
HALOGEN DOWNLIGHTER
FOR SMALL PLANTS

11 Thorn D Compact Fluorescent
A variation on number 10.

12 Philips Durable Compact Fluorescent
This fluorescent lamp is the tough outdoor version of numbers 10 and 11 above; it is protected by a glass sleeve. PAR lamps are also much used outdoors because they are made from cast glass which is very tough.

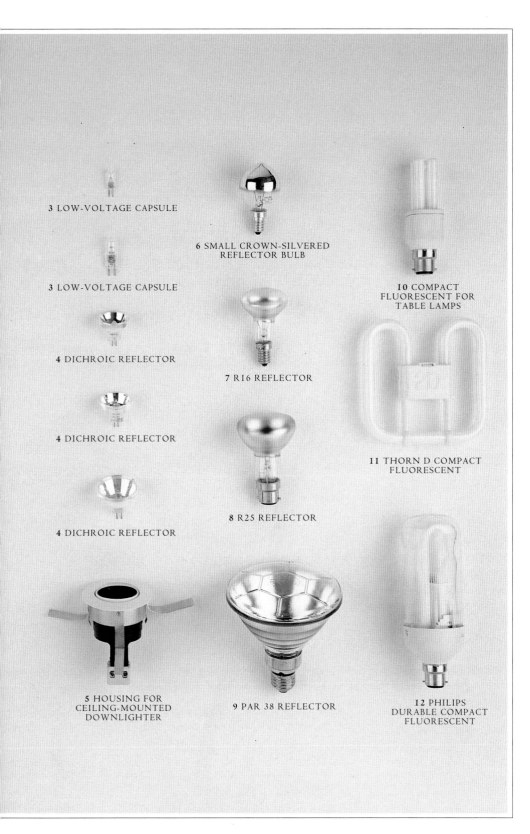

3 LOW-VOLTAGE CAPSULE

3 LOW-VOLTAGE CAPSULE

4 DICHROIC REFLECTOR

4 DICHROIC REFLECTOR

4 DICHROIC REFLECTOR

5 HOUSING FOR CEILING-MOUNTED DOWNLIGHTER

6 SMALL CROWN-SILVERED REFLECTOR BULB

7 R16 REFLECTOR

8 R25 REFLECTOR

9 PAR 38 REFLECTOR

10 COMPACT FLUORESCENT FOR TABLE LAMPS

11 THORN D COMPACT FLUORESCENT

12 PHILIPS DURABLE COMPACT FLUORESCENT

112 CONTEMPORARY TABLE LAMPS

Modern table lighting is a far cry from the single traditional standard lamp. Although period brass and glass library table lamps and Victorian-style bracketed table lamps are still reproduced, their lighting capabilities are limited in comparison with modern designs. This selection explores the effects produced by mixing light with glass, metal and plastic.

1 Glass Spiral Lamp
Designed by Clare Thatcher, this lamp is, essentially, a decorative uplighter/wall-washer, but it also creates pattern and interest on its own glass surface.

2 Small Oval Table Lamp
Made by Fontana Arte and designed by Daniela Puppa, this small lamp demonstrates the clever development of having both the stem and shade made from glass, then housing the light source in the stem. The elegant result is improved by squashing the shape of the lamp in plan into an oval.

3 Bestlite
The original Bestlite, designed by Robert Best, has been produced by Best and Lloyd since 1950. It is still, decades on, the simplest, most elegant version of a practical task light.

4 Mitre Lamp
Another Clare Thatcher lamp, this mitre lamp consists of a metal cone secured with rivets sitting on an elegant base. It provides both decoration and a subtle uplight for a table top.

5 Tango Desk Lamp
Made by Arteluce and designed by S Copeland, this is a piece whose form and decoration are more important than its function. It is designed to look good whether switched on or off. (Even its glass shade permits no transfer of light through it.) Beneath the limb-like construction, with its hooded head and visceral detailing, it functions in the same way as a standard adjustable table lamp.

6 Miss Sissi
This tiny table lamp designed by Philippe Starck is destined to become a classic; it is classically proportioned, yet much reduced in decoration and form. It is also affordable and very effective.

7 TA Table Light
Designed by Peter Nelson, this light dates from the 1960s and is a cool, minimal task light for a restrained setting. Its height and swivel are adjustable.

8 Jielde Work Lamp
Another perennial classic, this French industrial bench lamp looks like an Anglepoise on steroids.

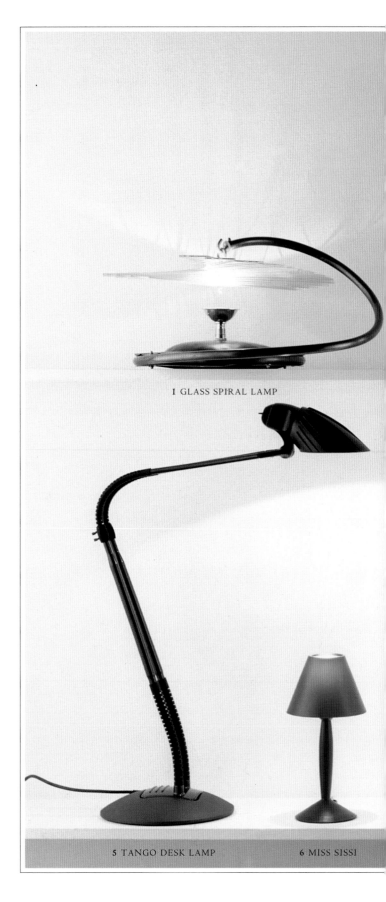

1 GLASS SPIRAL LAMP

5 TANGO DESK LAMP

6 MISS SISSI

2 SMALL OVAL TABLE LAMP   **3 BESTLITE**   **4 MITRE LAMP**

7 TA TABLE LIGHT   **8 JIELDE WORK LAMP**

114 TRADITIONAL TABLE LAMPS

The table lamp is the most underrated lighting accessory in the home, as it offers task and accent lighting that is both mobile and local to a specific activity. Because the light source is generally placed at eye level, a shade will always be necessary to reduce glare and direct the light towards the task or lit object. But the height of table lamps in a room has another, more psychological implication. Because we find ourselves closer to the light source, we feel warmed by it and the combination of uplight and shaded glow is reminiscent of the primitive fireside.

SHADING
Because of the size of the shade and its impact as the glowing element of the piece, it is vital to combine the aesthetics of the shade with the lamp. Shades of different size and angle cast different throws of light – the wider the angle of the shade, the wider the pool of light cast. This can also be altered by raising or lowering the shade relative to the lightbulb; a lightbulb positioned low in the shade will cast a large pool of light below.

USES VERSUS AESTHETICS
Although the maximum strength of bulb permitted in a mains-voltage table lamp is 60 watts, this is usually ample for most tasks or decorative effects. The next issue of most concern is the lamp's aesthetic design – how well it fits a room's decoration.

1 Storm Lantern
A seductively shaped glass bell used to shield candles or electric lamps.

2 Empire Lamp
A shallow shade with a wide angle offers a maximum throw of light.

3 Tôle Lamp
An opaque shade such as this one made of steel or tin gives an excellent source of localized light with no glare. Ideal for local illumination in a study.

4 Silver Candlestick and Shade
The prettiest decorative effects for candles are achieved by using pierced shades. The resulting effect is of light dancing on nearby surfaces.

5 Rise and Fall Lamp
This lamp is a good compromise of function and form where a lamp needs to serve several precise functions, for example in the middle of a room next to a sofa where it is used for reading and for general illumination. It has an extendable tube which rises, allowing a much greater area of the room to be lit.

6 Turned Wood Lamp
The use of a small shade on a turned wooden base gives this lamp a modern, quirky character.

7 Gothic Lamp
A strongly themed table lamp, its wide shade and its height make it ideal for placing to the rear of a large desk, from where it will happily illuminate the whole working surface.

8 Corinthian Lamp
A classic and classical design in terms of its potential as part of a well-designed scheme.

1 STORM LANTERN

5 RISE AND FALL LAMP

6 TURNED WOOD LAMP

2 EMPIRE LAMP

3 TÔLE LAMP

4 SILVER CANDLESTICK
AND SHADE

7 GOTHIC LAMP

8 CORINTHIAN LAMP

116 CONTEMPORARY WALL LIGHTS

Of all the types of modern lighting available today, wall lights offer the widest variety of design and effect. Their proximity to the wall means that they can utilize all the flat surface on which to create effects, offering sometimes extremely localized lighting. The six examples illustrated here offer effects far removed from the twinkle of period fittings, maximizing the potential of the electric light bulb as the light source.

1 Quarto Uplighter
Designed by Tobia Scarpa and manufactured by Flos, this simple uplighter is cleverly mounted clear of the wall to allow a spill of light from around the shape, cleverly throwing it into silhouette. The lense top efficiently directs the light reflected in the bowl onto the ceiling, for a highly ambient effect.

2 Carlton Bathroom Fitting
This piece by Pierre Yves Rochon meets regulations for bathrooms by housing the lamp in a sealed unit. The large diffusing filter contains a fluorescent tube that casts a soft low-glare light.

3 2739 VOR
Daniela Puppa's design is simple but breathtakingly effective. It consists of a back assembly for wall mounting, and a piece of circular frosted glass with a central hole. The third essential component is a crown-silvered lightbulb placed in the middle.

4 Clarus Picture Light
This discreet fitting manufactured by BETEC, contains a chain of tiny tungsten capsule lamps arranged in a row. The effect is rather weak, but sufficient to accent any nearby painting or object.

5 Luci Fair
Another Flos lamp, this one is designed by Philippe Starck. It makes a startlingly simple statement, projecting at an angle into the room like a horn. A slit in the glass cowl directs heat and light upwards.

6 Bit Parete No 5
Part of a collection of similar designs, this funky and fluid design in glass comes with flex and an in-line switch, so it can be hung on a wall and plugged in to a socket. It is designed by Ferruccio Laviani and manufactured by Foscarini.

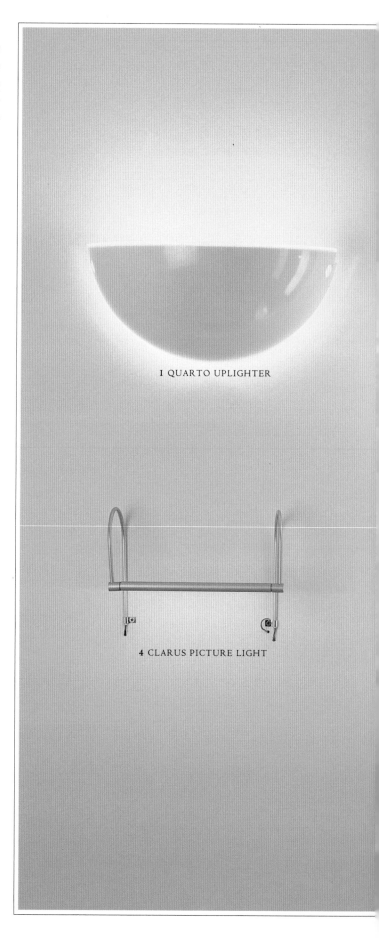

1 QUARTO UPLIGHTER

4 CLARUS PICTURE LIGHT

2 CARLTON
BATHROOM
FITTING

3 2739 VOR

5 LUCI FAIR

6 BIT PARETE NO 5

118 PERIOD WALL LIGHTS

To fully integrate a period light fitting into a decorative scheme, you should consider carefully its design, colour, finish and light output in relation to other elements in the room.

Throughout the 19th century, lamps were manufactured to burn either oil or gas and so were fitted with glass shades that were often etched to diffuse the light.

1 Leaf Sconce
This delicate metal uplighter houses an ordinary GLS bulb to wash the wall with light and sparkle through the leaves.

2 Rococo Sconce
A small, classic 18th-century design which has been much produced. For maximum effect, choose the wilder designs.

3 Gothic Uplighter
This uplighter allows the light from a 100-watt reflector bulb to be directed mainly towards the ceiling.

4 Biedermeier Uplighter
A traditional housing contains a powerful modern 100-watt mains-voltage halogen tube to fully illuminate a ceiling. This fitting would be equally at home in a Regency or Empire setting.

5 17th-century Tin Girandole
Up until the end of the 18th century, wall sconces and girandoles (sconces with a backing mirror) always took can-

dles. Consequently, they look happier in a contemporary setting if fitted with discreet low-wattage bulbs or individual small shades fitted over conventional candle bulbs.

6 Exterior Wall Lantern
Always ensure that a lamp situated outdoors is specifically designed for the purpose and that, when specified, it is not exposed directly to the wet.

7 Regency/Empire Sconce A resin copy of a somewhat hefty early 19th-century carved wooden original.

8 Gothic Sconce
The maximum wattage bulb for a wall fitting is 60 watts when using a conventional tungsten bulb. The output is severely reduced when the source is shaded but, for extra light, consider fitting a sconce with three, four or more arms.

1 LEAF SCONCE

2 ROCOCO SCONCE

6 EXTERIOR WALL LANTERN

3 GOTHIC UPLIGHTER

4 BIEDERMEIER UPLIGHTER

5 17th-CENTURY TIN GIRANDOLE

7 REGENCY/EMPIRE SCONCE

8 GOTHIC SCONCE

120 DECORATIVE CHANDELIERS

In period decoration it is not always necessary to include antique or even reproduction lighting pieces in your scheme. The important central position of a chandelier (or electrolier, the correct term for an electric lamp version) on a ceiling can be exploited by using a strongly thematic fitting.

1 Armillary Sphere
This modern McCloud & Co design based on 17th-century models of the universe, also known as Orreries, is a loose, thematic interpretation of a traditional form, whereas the Dutch chandelier (No 4, below) is a straight reproduction. The finish of dribbled verdigris adds resonance to its historical references.

2 Crown
Apart from its strong medieval theme, this McCloud & Co piece demonstrates a clever use of combination lighting. Inside is a mains-voltage halogen bulb serving two purposes; as an uplighter providing strong ambient light from the middle of the room (a useful trick in interiors where the wall decoration cannot be disturbed to route cabling for wall-mounted lights), and as a gentle downlighter through coloured oiled decorative paper mounted as a screen across the base of the chandelier. The bulbs mounted in glass candle tubes around the piece (see page 126) serve mainly as decoration.

3 Crystal Electrolier
This Italian design has more metal, and therefore more beef, than the traditional Austrian-Czechoslovak designs that date from the early 18th century onwards.

However, whichever type you choose, maximize the wonderful prismatic effects that crystal can create by looking for Strass or other high quality lead crystal.

4 Flemish Chandelier
This chandelier faithfully reproduces a traditional Dutch design dating from the 17th century. It was much used in Jacobean, Colonial and Queen Anne interiors, so many pewter and cheap rustic tin versions were made at the time. The qualities to look for in a modern version are a solid, large ball at the bottom, a generous florid design and a pale brass colour with finish that resembles the hand polishing on a cherished heirloom. Spray lacquer is often used to seal reproduction pieces, but it does not produce the same effect at all.

5 Montgolfier
Like the Armillary Sphere, this piece is both decorative and thematic.

6 Lantern
Based originally on Near Eastern hanging lanterns, this popular design offers an unobtrusive solution to the problem of lighting hallways in 18th- and 19th-century houses.

1 ARMILLARY SPHERE

4 FLEMISH CHANDELIER

2 CROWN

3 CRYSTAL
ELECTROLIER

6 LANTERN

5 MONTGOLFIER

1 TRIPLO EXPANDED
LINE KIT

3 SPUN ALUMINIUM
PENDANT

2 VELICA PENDANT

4 KELMSCOT
PENDANT

5 CRISOL PENDANT

The central pendant fitting as supplied by builders to most domestic rooms has had a bad press for a long time, because of its unflattering light and uncompromising position. The pieces illustrated here overcome these problems, either through their inherent style or through their clever ability to control the direction and quality of emitted light.

1 Triplo Expanded Line Kit
This assembly, designed by King, Miranda and Arnaldi and manufactured by Arteluce, has an integral transformer that powers three 12-volt tungsten-halogen sources. The dichroic reflectors are positioned on stalks of varying lengths, allowing the sources to be pointed in any direction. Any reflector can be fitted, giving a choice of light spread; narrow, wide or flood.

2 Velica Pendant
Manufactured by Arteluce and designed by Pagani and Perversi, this design consists of a frosted glass 'boat' strung on a cradle. Inside is a mains-voltage halogen source. A perforated mesh platform below the lamp inside ensures that a small amount of light is allowed to filter down to illuminate the glass, while the majority of light produced is reflected upwards. The arms to the side contribute to the elegance of the design while holding the feed wires well away from the source, so eliminating strong shadows on the ceiling and walls.

3 Spun Aluminium Pendant
A very simple and lightweight fitting manufactured by Kriptonite in Italy. The opaque shade and recessed bulb make for a low-glare fitting with a very directional cast of light.

4 Kelmscot Pendant
Designed and manufactured by McCloud & Co, this piece reproduces a style of 20th-century fitting popular until the 1950s. The strengthened and armoured bronze flex obviates the need for a chain, and the fitting can be converted to accept halogen 12-volt sources.

5 Crisol Pendant
This small, low-voltage halogen fitting has found favour in offices and board rooms where it is often slung low over a table. It is effectively a downlighter, housing just one dichroic lamp. Backspill through the reflector illuminates the blue glass housing with a soft glow. It is designed by King, Miranda and Arnaldi and manufactured by Arteluce.

124 FLOOR-MOUNTED LAMPS

A floor-mounted lamp is the perfect quick solution for establishing ambient and task lighting — the bones of any lighting scheme. Although the traditional 1950s standard lamp has fallen from favour in recent years, floor-mounted lamps are one of the most useful adjuncts to a room's lighting scheme. They offer a highly mobile source of ambient uplight, accent light or downwards-focused task light. Because their height and directions are also often adjustable, they are a more flexible option than a combination of wall-mounted uplighters and table lamps.

1 Montjuic Floor Light

This immensely tall fitting designed by Santiago Calatrava for Artemide is the acme of elegant uplighters for ceilings, producing a high level of mains-voltage halogen light. Its thick, frosted bowl provides additional unspecific task lighting as well as making the piece a decorative object in its own right.

2 Brera 134

Achille Castiglione's minimal lamp provides task or accent lighting by illuminating the space immediately around it. Its large frosted shade diffuses the light source, thus reducing glare.

3 Traditional Library Pedestal Lamp

This classic design has a pleated silk shade which diffuses the light source. The size of the aperture in the shade allows for the insertion of high-technology lighting components such as a reflector spotlamp or a PAR 38 spot, which acts as a ceiling uplighter.

4 FLA Footlight

Designed by Peter Nelson for Architectural Lighting, this versatile light can be placed on shelves or tables as a table lamp, or used on floors behind furniture to provide wallwash or accent lighting.

5 23/50 Low-voltage Footlight

Another footlight by the same designer, this smaller version is equally flexible: in addition to the uses outlined above, it can be installed on the top of cupboards to uplight ceilings as a source of ambient light. Most of the incidental 'special effects' shown in the case studies of this book were achieved with one of these Architectural Lighting fittings.

6 36/50 Low-voltage Floor Lamp

Also by Peter Nelson, this floor lamp is ideal as a mobile task or accent light.

1 MONTJUIC FLOOR LIGHT

2 BRERA 134

3 TRADITIONAL
LIBRARY PEDESTAL
LAMP

4 F L A
FOOTLIGHT

5 23/50
LOW-VOLTAGE
FOOTLIGHT

6 36/50
LOW-VOLTAGE
FLOOR LAMP

126 **ELECTRIC CANDLES**

In the quest for a perfect imitation of the natural candle, lighting designers have gone to ridiculous lengths to arrive at a passable substitute. But why? Perhaps it is the symbolic value of the candle as the light of life that is so admired. Certainly on period fittings, the scale and aesthetic appeal of these reproduction electric candles offer an elegant alternative to the real thing.

1 Halogen Halo
To combine a high light output with the warm effect of translucent wax, a 25-watt halogen capsule is mounted discreetly inside a fireproof glass tube. This McCloud & Co unit is sold as one and contains a transformer and electronics that give a random flicker and a 'moving light' effect which responds to wind or low-frequency sound.

2 Glass Candle
A smaller McCloud & Co tube, this one can be used with mains-voltage 25-watt candle bulbs. It performs the task of a shade, diffusing the light through its acid-etched surface.

3 Glass Candle
A slightly different version of 2, above, note how the top edge of the tube catches the light, simulating molten wax.

4 Acrylic Candle
This French acrylic candle takes a tiny E10 screw-in bulb, allowing the form of the candle to be tapered.

5 Card Candle Tube
This is the traditional, economical form of imitation candle bulb. It is often decorated with drips for true cartoon effect.

6 Flicker Flame
This ingenious mains-voltage lamp comes from Sweden. Its design relies on clever electronics, producing a low output of light from a bulb on a stalk which wobbles every few seconds in response to magnetic pulses. It slots into a standard SES fitting.

1 HALOGEN HALO   2 GLASS CANDLE

3 GLASS CANDLE

4 ACRYLIC CANDLE

5 CARD CANDLE TUBE

6 FLICKER FLAME

128 **CANDLES**

Never leave lit candles unattended in a room. When you blow out a candle, put your hand behind it to catch the tiny gobbets of wax that will otherwise solidify on your table. Always pinch the wick with moistened fingers immediately afterwards, to prevent it from smoking and giving off the unmistakable smell of burnt cotton and fat.

1 Tallow Candle
The design of these candles, made from pure beef dripping, has not changed for hundreds of years. Their high grease content and unpleasant odour mean that they are no longer in common use.

2 Pure Stearin Household Candles
These standard domestic candles are made in a mould using a 150-year-old recipe. They comprise stearin (stearic acid) extracted from tallow. Extremely popular, they burn very cleanly.

3 Decorative Candles
Screen-printed and gold twist candles make interesting embellishments for traditional wall sconces.

4 Citronella Insect Repellant Outdoor Candle
These highly scented candles should only be used outdoors, as their emissions can be unpleasant for humans as well as insects if used in confined spaces.

5 Hand-dipped and Rolled Church Candle
This traditional altar candle is formed according to a method first used by the Romans, whereby successive dippings of a single wick in hot wax builds up layer after layer, and slowly a candle is created.

6 'Honeycomb' Candles
Although these candles appear to be made from sheet honeycomb, it is impossible to find large enough flawless sheets to make them. In reality, they are made from a mixture of waxes which are pressed into flat sheets and then rolled up.

7 25% Beeswax, 75% Stearin Church Candles
Although originally made for churches only, these slightly more expensive candles are now popular with domestic users. They burn slowly and cleanly and give off a pleasant honeyed smell. The 25% minimum beeswax content is still dictated by a Papal bull.

8 Reamer for Large Candles
These tools are used nowadays only for the manufacture of large church candles. They gouge out a deep hole in the base of the candle to prevent it from splitting when it is pushed onto the spike, or pricket.

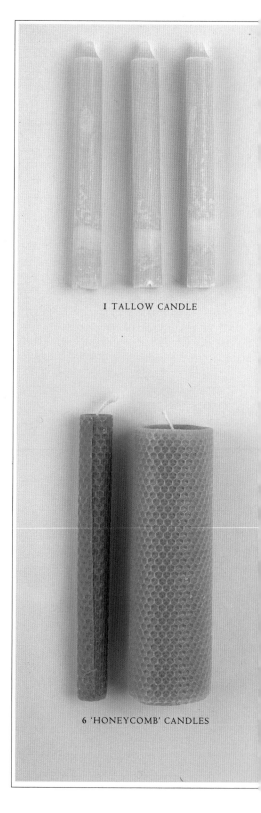

1 TALLOW CANDLE

6 'HONEYCOMB' CANDLES

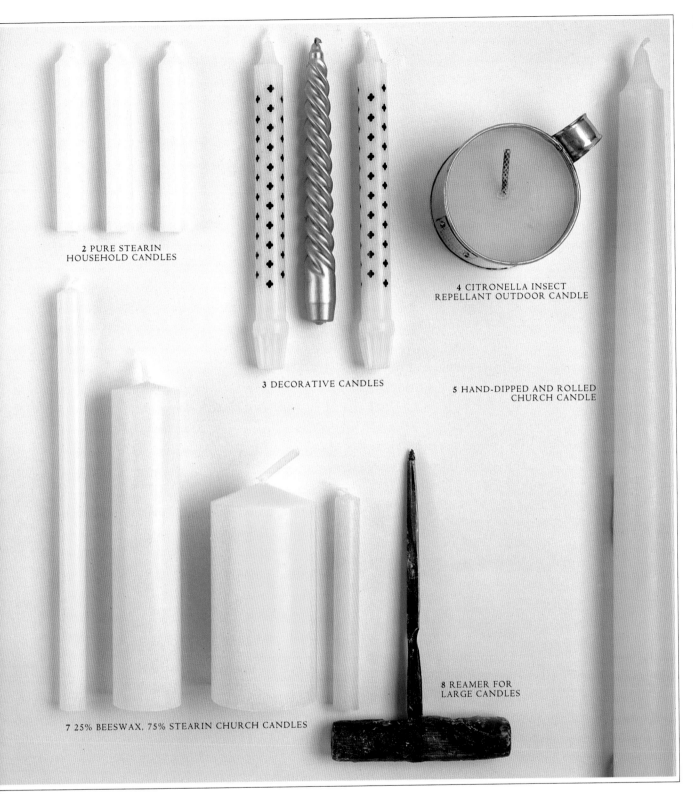

**2 PURE STEARIN
HOUSEHOLD CANDLES**

3 DECORATIVE CANDLES

**4 CITRONELLA INSECT
REPELLANT OUTDOOR CANDLE**

**5 HAND-DIPPED AND ROLLED
CHURCH CANDLE**

**8 REAMER FOR
LARGE CANDLES**

7 25% BEESWAX, 75% STEARIN CHURCH CANDLES

130 LAMPSHADES

The glare of a light source can be softened considerably be means of shading or shielding. If an opaque shade is used it will also serve as a reflector, bouncing light in a particular direction. But it is surprising how even a shade made from a translucent material like silk or oiled card will serve to 'direct' the light, its internal surfaces allowing maybe only 25 or 30 per cent of light through, while reflecting the rest out. For comparison, look at the traditional table lamps on page 114.

1 Damask Half Shield for Wall Lights
Silk responds well to being back lit, and is provided in a wide range of textures. See 2 and 7 below, for different effects.

2 Gothic Silk Shade
A traditional shade, this quatrefoil design made from damask silk is specially designed to achieve perfect period authenticity.

3 1920s' Shaped Pleated Shade
Here silk has been very tightly pleated to form a traditional fabric shade.

4 Traditional Parchment Coolie
Parchment or parchment paper shades project a warm 'antique light'.

5 Wall Light Shades
These McCloud & Co wall light shades are only half-round to allow light to be reflected against the wall.

6 Improvised Shade
Lampshades improvised from found materials offer the most exciting way of playing with lighting, to direct it, make it perform and incorporate it into a decorative scheme.

Baking and patisserie tins make excellent reflectors, particularly if placed one inside the other. When experimenting with homemade shades, do be sure to consult a qualified electrician to check that what you are doing is safe.

7 Silk-wrapped Shade
A strong contrast to the traditional silk lampshade, this version has a crumpled quality which has been achieved by soaking silk in glue and leaving it to stiffen on a spiral-wound frame.

8 Hollophane Pressed Glass Shade
This shade fractures the light source by refracting it down the length of its grooves, thus reducing glare.

9 Moulded Glass Shades (for low voltage)
Glass is the most valuable material for shading light, as shades can be made in an infinite variety of texture, colour and translucency.

10 Oiled Wallpaper
This 'lampshade' is in fact improvized from a coil of lining paper oiled with linseed oil (see page 133).

1 DAMASK HALF SHIELD FOR WALL LIGHTS

4 TRADITIONAL PARCHMENT COOLIE

7 SILK-WRAPPED SHADE

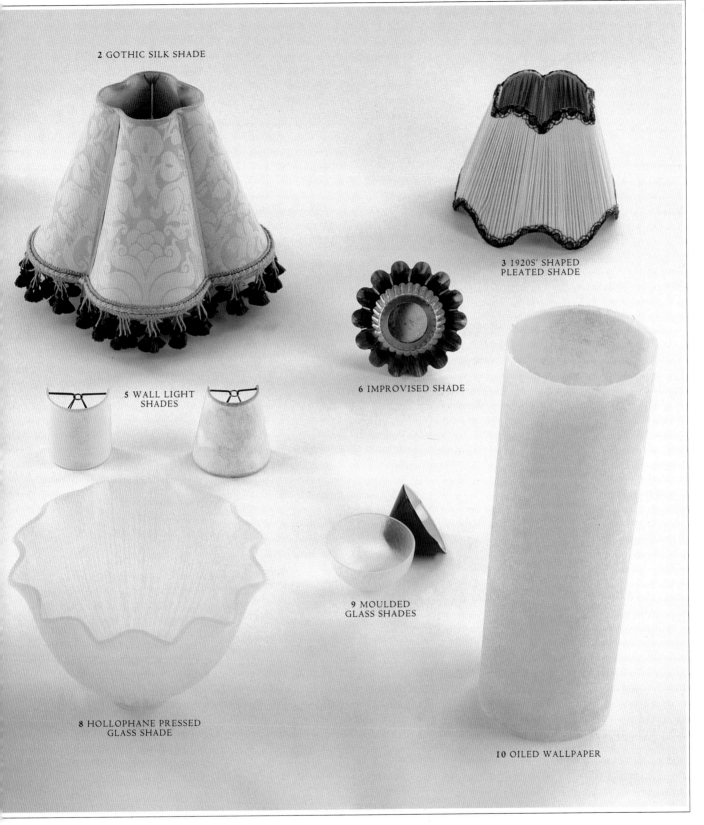

2 GOTHIC SILK SHADE

3 1920S' SHAPED
PLEATED SHADE

5 WALL LIGHT
SHADES

6 IMPROVISED SHADE

9 MOULDED
GLASS SHADES

8 HOLLOPHANE PRESSED
GLASS SHADE

10 OILED WALLPAPER

2 BRASS MESH

3 BRONZE MESH
ON SHADE

1 FINE STAINLESS
STEEL MESH

9 SAMPLES OF CAST GLASS

12 BEADED GLASS SHEET
– HALF SANDBLASTED

13 TRADITIONAL STAINED
GLASS IN LEAD 'CAME'

10 CRYSTALS

14 CAST GREEN
'BLOB',
CRAFTSMAN MADE

11 GLASS BEADS OR NUGGETS

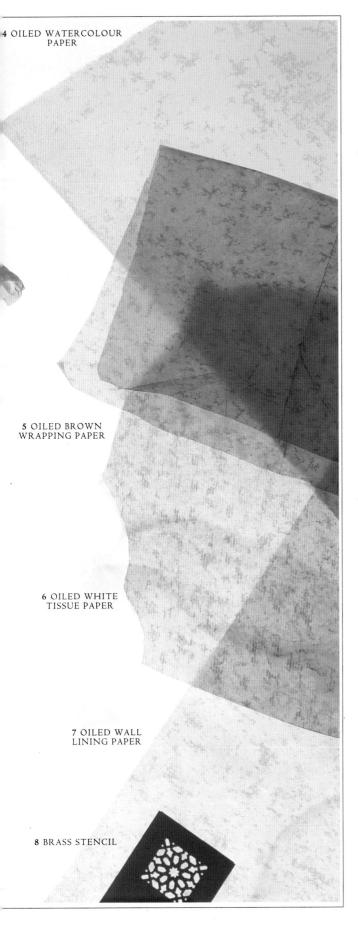

4 OILED WATERCOLOUR
PAPER

5 OILED BROWN
WRAPPING PAPER

6 OILED WHITE
TISSUE PAPER

7 OILED WALL
LINING PAPER

8 BRASS STENCIL

GLASS, FILTERS AND OTHER MATERIALS 133

Conventional shades and light fittings can be transformed by the use of unusual objects and different fittings. But remember.to consult a qualified electrician before experimenting. Close shading of a light source can cause heat build-up resulting in fire or the failure of the lamp. Paper is, of course, highly flammable, while metal conducts electricity.

The best solution is to use these materials over other, already existing forms of shading such as half drums designed for wall lights.

I Fine Stainless Steel Mesh
Meshes filter the light and alter its quality. They are available from industrial filter manufacturers, but can also be garnered from old hi-fi speakers.

2 Brass Mesh
This mesh offers a translucent barrier to the light and as such, reflects a certain amount of light, resulting in heat build-up if placed too close to a source. Placed under a pendant fitting it reflects a good proportion of the light onto the ceiling as ambient light, whilst permitting some diffused light to pass through.

3 Bronze Mesh on Shade
The easiest way to use mesh is over existing shades; it can be easily bent around them.

4 Oiled Watercolour Paper
Virtually any paper, even heavy watercolour paper, can be oiled to make it translucent and tough.

5 Oiled Brown Wrapping Paper
To oil paper, rub both sides with a cloth that has been soaked in boiled linseed oil and wipe off the excess. Hang up the paper in a warm place to dry. It should take 2-3 days.

6 Oiled White Tissue Paper
When you have oiled your paper, stick it to your chosen shade with oil-based varnish.

7 Oiled Wall Lining Paper
The cheapest paper available makes wonderful translucent shading material.

8 Brass Stencil
This stencil provides an opaque barrier to the light, a new use for a discarded decorative tool.

9 Samples of Cast Glass

10 Crystals
Available from craft shops and specialist glass manufacturers, these crystals can also be found by dismantling second-hand light fittings.

11 Glass Beads or Nuggets
These are made by dropping liquid glass into water. They are useful for filling otherwise plain glass jars for backlighting and placing on window sills.

12 Beaded Glass Sheet - Half Sandblasted
This sheet shows the translucent effects obtainable by acid etching or sandblasting glass.

13 Traditional Stained Glass in Lead 'Came'
A traditional, if somewhat heavy technique, stained glass is best used in windows and large flat areas incorporated into large chandeliers or ceiling panels.

14 Cast Green 'Blob', Craftsman Made
This example utilizes the liquid appearance of glass to its maximum.

Working with an Electrician

The first step when planning your lighting should ideally be at the stage when you are still choosing your colours, fabrics and papers. The messy business of chasing cables and conduits into walls and behind ceilings should be carried out before decorating.

Unless you are competent and experienced, do not try to tackle domestic wiring, always consult a reputable electrician. Electrics is the one area of house maintenance best not tackled by the DIY enthusiast. The consequences can be lethal, not just for the installer but also for an innocent user.

The installation of wiring and fittings is governed by a lengthy list of regulations to prevent the risk of shock, heat build-up and fire. Find an electrician who is a member of a national regulatory body (see Registered Bodies, page 142), and insist on written quotes and invoices, which will be necessary to retain in the event that you need to seek recourse against them. Approach at least two, if not three, electricians to submit separate quotes.

It is important that you give each of them an identical specification. Talk to them first on the telephone and discuss the job in as much detail as possible. Note any relevant points that each of them may make, asking their advice where necessary.

Use these notes as the basis for a written specification and ask one of the electricians to your house, preferably the most helpful. Again, keep the notebook handy and follow him around your home, taking down any points he makes. Finally, use all the information

you have gathered to brief the other two electricians as specifically as possible. This way, you will arrive at the highest possible specification and be able to choose the most competitive quote.

Of course, you may choose to use a professional lighting designer.

The listings on page 142 will provide you with the names of several well established lighting design companies who specialize in domestic work. They offer an initial consultancy for very reasonable rates, but will also provide fittings and supervise installation.

SAFETY

When specifying fittings or briefing an electrician, never be tempted to compromise the safety of what you are doing. Check that your electrician knows the regulations concerning bathroom fittings and external lighting. Here are some guidelines:

1. Any luminaire installed in a bathroom must be at least 2.5m ($2^1/_3$yds) away from the bath or shower (this is impossible in most bathrooms unless the metal parts are totally enclosed in a sealed unit or are made untouchable in a shielding frame).

2. Many manufacturers, local authorities and commercial installers insist that low-voltage lighting circuits mounted in a ceiling must include protective heat shields around each fitting to prevent a fire risk. Even then, some authorities will not allow the installation of such circuits in particularly old buildings where dirt and dust between narrowly spaced joists in ceiling spaces pose serious hazards.

3. Low-voltage supplies to tungsten-halogen garden lighting can be run overground, but the cables must be of the special heatproof variety. There are regulations covering the siting, protection and ventilation of transformers.

4. Mains-voltage garden lighting must take its supply from a special armoured cable buried at least 45cm (18in) underground. Alternatively, overhead lighting can be fed by a suspended cable which must be hung at 3.5m (11ft) minimum and supported every 3.5m (11ft).

5. Exterior lights (luminaires) should be marked with an IP (ingress protection) code, consisting of 2 numbers. The first, on a scale of 0-6, deals with how mechanically insulated it is against persons or dust. The second deals with how waterproof it is, ranging from 0, zero protection, through drip, splash, rain and jet proof to 8, meaning that the fitting is capable of being permanently submerged in water at pressure.

What Light Is

Our perception of light and how we see the world is controlled by the sensitivity of our retinas. Light is composed of electromagnetic radiation, as are gamma rays, radio waves, infra-red, x-rays, and ultra-violet waves. If our eyes were sensitive enough, we would see a world 'lit' by all these forms of radiation. But we only perceive a tiny slice of the whole electromagnetic spectrum.

All forms of radiation are measured in wavelengths, literally the physical length of one 'pulse' of the radiation, and the unit of measurement is the nanometer, or one millionth of a millimetre. Light occupies a band between 380 and 760 nanometers. Immediately below 380 and stretching down to 100 nanometers is ultra-violet radiation, and above 760 stretching way up to a wavelength of a tenth of a millimetre, is infra-red. Some idea of the vastness of the hidden spectrum beyond can be gleaned when you realize that your stereo picks up radio waves (composed of the same radiation as light), that can have a wavelength of 250 metres.

HOW WARM OR COLD IS YOUR LIGHTING?

Natural daylight is the benchmark by which most people gauge artificial lighting. The quality of natural daylight can vary wildly between the pure white light of direct sunlight at midday to the bluish tones of light reflected from a northern blue sky into, for example, a north facing room.

The chart to the right illustrates the colour of light as emitted from both natural and artificial light sources. This

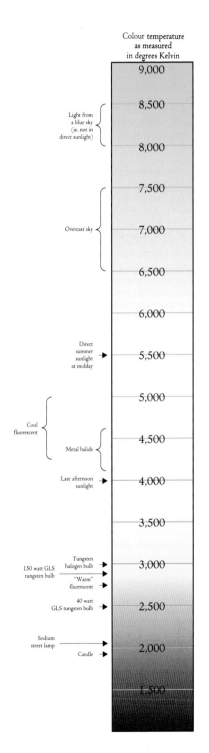

Colour temperature as measured in degrees Kelvin

9,000

8,500 — Light from a blue sky (ie. not in direct sunlight)

8,000

7,500

7,000 — Overcast sky

6,500

6,000

5,500 — Direct summer sunlight at midday

5,000

4,500 — Cool fluorescent — Metal halide

4,000 — Late afternoon sunlight

3,500

3,000 — Tungsten halogen bulb — 150 watt GLS tungsten bulb — "Warm" fluorescent

2,500 — 40 watt GLS tungsten bulb

2,000 — Sodium street lamp — Candle

1,500

is a useful guide in planning the association of lighting and colour in decorative schemes. The scale is marked in degrees Kelvin, a term used to denote the 'colour temperature' of light. Broadly speaking, it is comparable to heating a bar of iron in a flame. It passes from black to cherry red then bright red. As the bar gets hotter still, it slowly turns yellow and then finally 'white hot'. At this point the colour temperature of the bar may be around 4000 degrees Kelvin (corresponding to the white area on the chart).

Tungsten-halogen lighting has, for years, been the preferred choice for display and restaurant-table lighting because it gives a cool, almost white light. Food, for example, looks more appetizing under halogen than under warm fluorescents, which give it a magenta pink cast.

But metal halide lighting will soon be available for domestic fittings (many cars are now being fitted with 12-volt metal halide lamps) and it gives a much purer white light. Even cool fluorescent tubes offer a whiter alternative, although their colour is often unpleasantly 'spiked' with a great deal of yellowish green.

(LEFT) *This Kelvin temperature chart shows us how we perceive light. A cool fluorescent may appear perfectly white when looking at it (as it is recorded on the Kelvin chart), but it is its spectral analysis as shown overleaf which reveals the true story, and helps us understand why some colours, including skin tones, can look ghastly under fluorescent lighting.*

WHICH TYPE OF LIGHT?
The colour illustrations on the chart below show how different types of natural and artificial light are composed. For simplified purposes, the discernible spectrum is made up of the colours in the rainbow.

If bright sunshine is taken and broken up (refracted) through a lens, such as the effect seen in a rainbow — where myriad water droplets do the same thing — the result is an obvious range of the seven colours red, orange, yellow, green, blue, indigo and violet. An equal quantity of each makes pure white light. But if a prism is held in front of a tungsten bulb, the resulting colours consist of mainly red or yellow. So the illustrations below are simply a breakdown of the composition of the light that each type of light source gives out.

COLOUR OF LIGHT | DESCRIPTION | HOW IT WORKS

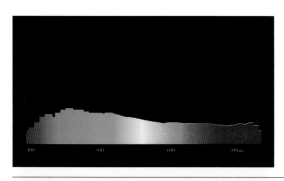

BRIGHT NATURAL DAYLIGHT

Daylight

A 'full spectrum' light (direct sunlight) where all the constituent colours of white light are more or less evenly balanced.

Direct sunlight punches straight through the atmosphere.

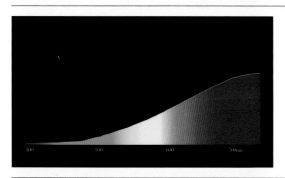

NORTHERN LIGHT

Daylight

A bluish light occurring from overall illumination from a sunless blue sky to the north.

The particles of the atmosphere refract direct sunlight filtering out the warmer colours and allowing more blue light through.

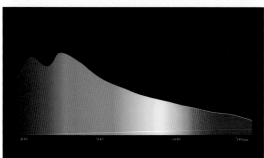

ORDINARY TUNGSTEN BULB

Incandescent light (produced by heating a filament)

Familiar standard form of domestic lighting producing a very 'warm' light.

Type of light that is produced by a tungsten filament that glows when an electrical current is passed through it. The filament is contained in a gas or vacuum.

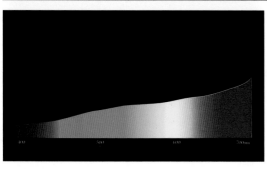

TUNGSTEN-HALOGEN LIGHT

Incandescent light (produced by heating a filament)

A whiter light of greater perceivable intensity than ordinary tungsten light. Low voltage versions are popular.

A tungsten filament burns in halogen gas, at a higher temperature than ordinary tungsten. The light is therefore whiter (see Kelvin chart on page 135).

For example, the illustration for fluorescent light overleaf (common discharge light) shows orangey-pink and yellowy-green spikes; these correlate with our perception of fluorescent as unpleasant and sharp, a light that distorts the colours of what we see.

(BELOW AND OVERLEAF) *Which type of light? With this chart you can see what type of light is created by both natural daylight and various types of artificial light sources ranging from an incandescent light source to a high-pressure mercury lamp.*

(PAGES 140-141) *The* Which Light Bulb? *chart then takes you one step further, as it outlines the size, quality, efficiency and principle uses of more than 25 different types of bulb. Through using it you will more easily find a bulb that is exactly right for your requirements.*

REMARKS	ADVANTAGES	DISADVANTAGES
The whitest, purest light known.		
It is remarkable how luminous a blue shirt looks in shadow on a sunny day!		
Flattering to skin tones and psychologically appealing.	* Easily dimmable * Suited to mains voltage * Available as GLS bulbs, PAR and reflector bulbs, decorative bulbs, and in colours * Cheap to buy	* Hot, subject to thermal shock (except PAR lamps) and therefore unsuitable for use as outside bulbs * Have short lives (1000hrs) * The least efficient of all light sources, therefore expensive to run * Glass blackens with age
Colours appear sharper under halogen.	* At low voltage, tungsten-halogen sources produce the same output as similarly rated mains-voltage tungsten bulbs * Extended life * No deterioration in light output (2-3000hrs) * Dimmable	* More heat generated than from tungsten, requiring use of heat-dispersing aids such as dichroic reflectors, heat-proof mountings, dust covers, etc * Low-voltage versions require transformers * Inefficient

138

COLOUR OF LIGHT	DESCRIPTION	HOW IT WORKS

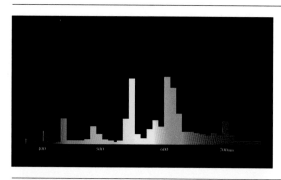

A TYPICAL FLUORESCENT

Common discharge light (a gas carries a current and excites a phosphorescing coating on glass)

A low-pressure discharge lamp producing light of very unequal composition often with green or pink emphasis.

Argon or Krypton gas in a tube excites a phosphorescing coating. The combination of phosphors determines the particular 'colour' of the tube.

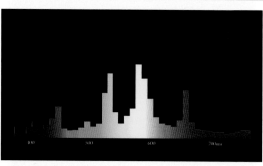

METAL HALIDE LIGHT

Specialized discharge light

A much more balanced light which although having 'spikes', has them spread across the spectrum.

A gas is excited by an arc passed between two cathodes. The presence of metal halides in the gas assist it in producing a discharge of light.

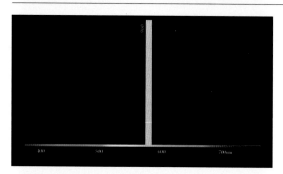

LOW-PRESSURE SODIUM LIGHT (street lighting)

Specialized discharge light

A bright yellow light of singular intensity.

An electric arc is struck between two electrodes held in a glass envelope filled with sodium vapour. The gas ionizes and produces light in response.

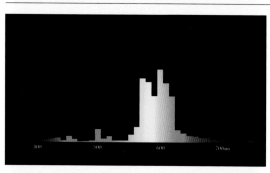

HIGH-PRESSURE SODIUM LIGHT (industrial and commercial use)

Specialized discharge light

Warm, orange-tinged light.

Like the low-pressure version, but the gas is contained at high pressure, providing a better range of frequencies.

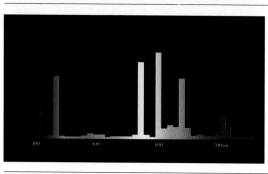

HIGH-PRESSURE MERCURY LAMP (industrial and commercial use)

Specialized discharge light

A light perceived as composed mainly of the blue, green, yellow and violet end of the spectrum.

Like the sodium lamp, but using mercury vapour at high pressure.

REMARKS	ADVANTAGES	DISADVANTAGES
Warm, cool, and special colour fluorescents are available.	* Cheap to run with extremely long life (8,000 hrs) * Compact versions available * Cool-running and therefore highly efficient, operating at up to 1/10th the cost of incandescent lighting * Shadowless light from a large source	* Requires a choke starter * Compact versions less efficient * Up to 25 different versions of white light versions on the market, all different * Disposal problems from toxic chemicals * Bland effect, flickering * Can only be dimmed using extra electronic ballasts
Not quite yet a viable product for domestic use.	* The nearest thing to daylight * Quite energy efficient, long lamp life * Compact bulbs	* Expensive to install with bulky control gear boxes necessary * Can appear sterile at night
By night, the human eye can respond to yellow frequencies much easier than any other, perceiving most things lit by it in monochrome, but clearly.	* Cheap and efficient to run * Most efficient light source available	* Bulky due to double-insulating glass envelope * Requires complicated electronic starting gear * Run-up time to strike full power is 10 minutes * Toxic materials mean serious disposal problems * Orange light * Loss of efficiency with age
Warm light, suitable for large commercial interiors.	* Reasonable light quality at extremely low cost	* Gives poor colour rendering * Risk of explosion * Bulky, needs electronic gear and a run-up time * Toxic materials, therefore disposal problems
Blue light suitable for commercial large-scale interiors. For better colour rendering, can be mixed with high-pressure sodium lighting.	* Reasonable light quality at extremely low cost.	* Gives poor colour rendering * Risk of explosion * Bulky, needs electronic gear and a run-up time * Toxic materials, therefore disposal problems

140 WHICH LIGHT BULB?

	TUNGSTEN BULBS	REFLECTOR BULBS	PAR LAMPS	FLUORESCENT TUBES
DIMENSIONS ARE GIVEN IN mm Ø = DIAMETER	1 150 watt Ø 60-80mm 2 25-100 watt Ø 45mm 3 pygmy Ø 26mm 4 candle Ø 30mm 5 globe Ø 60-75mm 6 appliance Ø 25-30mm 7 golfball Ø 45mm 8 length variable	9 10 crown-reflector Ø 45-65mm 11 reflector Ø 50-95mm 12 13	14 Ø 122mm	15 long tube length 20-240cm smaller narrow tubes are now available
WATTAGES AVAILABLE	15-200 watt	40-150 watt	60-150 watt	8-58 watt
BEAM ANGLE	non-specific	12°, 16°, 22°, 30°, 32°, 35°, 70° crown-silvered	12° spot-30° flood	N/A
LIGHT QUALITY	warm	warm	warm	mixed
ENERGY EFFICIENCY	poor	poor	poor	very good
LIFESPAN	1000 hrs (double life bulbs: 2000 hrs)	1000 hrs	2000 hrs	7000 hrs
PRINCIPLE USES	General lighting. Can be installed to produce any lighting type according to reflectors/diffusers used.	Accent, task and ambient lighting.	Accent, task, ambient and exterior lighting.	Ambient lighting; not dimmable.

COMPACT FLUORESCENT TUBES	MAINS-VOLTAGE HALOGEN	LOW-VOLTAGE HALOGEN BULBS	SPECIALIST LAMPS
16 'D' lamp 17 18 standard ∅ 12-70mm 19 glass protected ∅ 73mm	20 bayonet or ES fitting 45mm 21 tube fitting ∅ 20-23mm 22 dichroic reflector	23 capsule 24 capsule mounted in dichroic reflector	Note: all these lamps require specialist ancillary equipment and can be toxic in use and in disposal 25 High-pressure sodium, metal halide or mercury ∅ 55-90mm 26 sodium, mercury or metal halide tubular ∅ 32mm
7-36 watt	70-700 watt	15-50 watt	50-250 watt
N/A, although can be used with reflectors	N/A, unless used with reflectors	10°-60°	N/A
mixed	bright white	bright white	sodium: warm mercury: cold halide: white
very good (though not as good as long tubes)	poor	average	excellent (five times that of tungsten)
5000 hrs	5000 hrs	2000-3000 hrs	5000-10,000 hrs
Ambient, accent and decorative lighting; not dimmable.	Ambient, accent and task lighting.	Accent, task and decorative lighting.	Exterior, industrial, ambient and task lighting.

English

Practicalities

142 USEFUL ADDRESSES

Artemide GB Ltd.
17-19 Neal Street
London WC2H 9PU
0171 240 2552

Specializes in state-of-the-art, avant-garde decorative lighting. Mail order.

Atrium Ltd.
22-24 St. Giles High Street
London WC2H 8LN
0171 379 7288

Major importers and suppliers of designer light fitting ranges such as Flos, Artemide and The Lumen Center. Mail order.

Anglepoise Lighting
Unit 51
Enfield Industrial Estate
Redditch B97 6DR
01527 63771

Designers and manufacturers of a wide range of energy-efficient task and ambient light fittings.

Besselink & Jones
99 Walton Street
London SW3 2HH
0171 584 0343

Suppliers of contemporary and antique lighting, as well as hand-made lampshades. Services include conversions, repair, special finishes, and manufacture to order.

Best & Lloyd Ltd.
William Street West
Smethwick
Warley
West Midlands B66 2NX
0121 558 1191

Designers and manufacturers of brass decorative lighting, specializing in hand-made and traditional designs.

Beta Lighting Ltd.
383-387 Leeds Road
Bradford BD3 9LZ
01274 721129

Manufacturers and suppliers of commercial and architectural lighting, specializing in low-energy lighting solutions. Special manufacturing service. Mail order.

British Electric Lamps Ltd.
Spencer Hill Road
Wimbledon
London SW19 4EN
0181 946 5035

Suppliers of light bulbs and decorative light fittings.

Chelsom Ltd.
Heritage House
Clifton Road
Blackpool
Lancashire FY4 4QA
01253 791344
0171 736 2559 (London showroom)

Specialists in a wide range of modern and traditional designer lighting. Services include conversions, special finishes, restoration, design and manufacture.

Christopher Wray's Lighting Emporium
600 King's Road
London SW6 2YW
0171 371 8023

Specialists in reproduction Victorian lighting and a wide range of other fittings.

Concord Lighting
Avia Way
New Haven
East Sussex BN9 0ED
01273 515811

Manufacturers and designers of architectural and commercial lighting.

Davey Lighting
4 Oak Industrial Park
Chelmsford Road
Great Dunmow
Essex CM6 1XN
01371 873174

Specialists in classic antique boat light-fittings. Mail order.

Into Lighting
49 The High Street
Wimbledon Village
London SW19 5AX
0181 946 8533
General suppliers of a wide variety of lighting including exclusive imported ranges.

John Cullen Lighting
216 Fulham Palace Road
London W6 9NT
0171 381 8944

Specialists in the supply of discreet and original lighting products, both modern and traditional, designed to meet sophisticated interior design requirements. Mail order.

Lighting Design Ltd.
Lighting Design House
Ellaline Road
London W6 9NZ
0171 381 8999

Independent design consultants.

Lighting Design Partnership
45 Timber Bush
Leith
Edinburgh EH6 6QH
0131 553 6633

Independent design consultants.

London Lighting Company
133-135 Fulham Road
London SW3 6RT
0171 589 3612

Design-oriented retailers, specializing in modern lighting, including many exclusive ranges.

Marcatre
179-199 Shaftesbury Avenue
London WC2H 8AR
0171 379 6865

Suppliers of general office requirements, specializing in Arteluce and Flos lighting.

Maurice Brill Lighting Design
48 Chilton Street
London E2 6DZ
0171 613 0456

Independent design consultants.

McCloud and Co.
269 Wandsworth Bridge Road
London SW6 2TX
0171 371 7151

Manufacturers of original decorative and ambient lighting. Standard finishes, special designs and finishes to order. Catalogue £3. Mail order.

Shiu-Kaykan
34 Lexington Street
London WIR 3HR
0171 434 4095

Consultancy and design specialists. Mail order.

Vaughan Lighting
156 Wandsworth Bridge Road
London SW6 2UH
0171 731 3133

Specialists in antique and reproduction lighting.

West Midland Lighting Centre
10-12 York Road
Erdington
Birmingham B23 6TE
0121 350 1999

Suppliers of a whole range of decorative lighting.

REGISTERED BODIES

NICEIC
National Inspection Council for Electrical Installation Contracting
Vintage House
37 Albert Embankment
London SE1 7UG
0171 582 7746

ECA
Electrical Contractors Association
34 Palace Court
London W2 1HY
0171 229 1266

All qualified electricians should be members of either of these two bodies, both of which will investigate complaints made against their members.

IEE
Institution of Electrical Engineers
Savoy Place
London WC2 ROBL
0171 240 1871

This body sets down the wiring and installation regulations that the ECA and NICEIC uphold.

ACKNOWLEDGMENTS

The author would like to thank the following for their help in providing the locations used in this book: **Kate Dunwell** and **Katy Brown** for the hallways; **Ashley Lloyd-Jennings** for the living room; **Hamiltons Photographers**, 35 Fentiman Road, London SW8 for the kitchen; **Baer & Ingram Wallpapers**, 273 Wandsworth Bridge Road, London SW6 for the bedroom; **The Jacuzzi Whirlpool Bathroom Centre**, 255 Queenstown Road, London SW8 3NP for the bathroom; **Caroline Vernon** for One Room Five Ways.

Enormous thanks are due to **Sally Storey** and her company, **John Cullen Lighting Design**, 216 Fulham Palace Road, London W6 6NT, for allowing us to photograph in their showroom, offering guidance and help throughout and providing us with the locations for the dining room and garden chapters. Additional thanks are due to **Price's Candles**, **Vaughan Lighting**, **Besselink & Jones** and the **London Lighting Company** for their kind loan of luminaires.

Personal thanks must go to my friend Michael Crockett for his wonderful photography, my agent Jane Turnbull and all at Ebury Press who have made this book such a pleasure to write; and last but not least, to Sharon Kelly for her untiring work in helping to write this book.

The publisher thanks the following:
2-3 Marie Claire Maison/Nicolas Tosni/Julie Borgeaud;
4 Tim Street-Porter/Architect Brian Murphy;
6-7 Elizabeth Whiting & Associates/Neil Lorimer;
8-9 Marie Claire Maison/Deidi von Schaewen/Pascal Billaud;
10 above Bent Rej;
11 below Paul Ryan/International Interiors/designer Corinne Calesso;
12 below Bent Rej;
13 above left Elizabeth Whiting & Associates/Ed Ironside;
20 Absolute Action;
28 Paul Ryan/International Interiors/designer Charles Rutherfoord;
29 above left Stuart McIntyre;
29 above right Arcaid/Richard Bryant/designer Colin Gold;
30 The Interior World/Fritz von der Schulenburg/designer Gerard Bach;
31 Arcaid/Julie Phipps;
38 Hotze Eisma;
40-41 Paul Ryan/International Interiors/designer Bruno Boretti;
41 Paul Ryan/International Interiors/designer K Paakonen;
42 JB Visual Press/Horst Neumann;
43 The Interior World/Fritz von der Schulenburg/ Architect Andrea Cenci;
50 Paul Ryan/International Interiors/Architects Tigerman;
51 La Maison de Marie Claire/Gilles de Chabaneix/Catherine Ardouin;
52 Paul Ryan/International Interiors/Architects Smith-Miller/Hawkinson;
53 Stuart McIntyre;
54 Elizabeth Whiting & Associates/Peter Woloszynski;
55 The Interior World/Fritz von der Schulenburg (Andrew Wadsworth);
62 Elizabeth Whiting & Associates/Ed Ironside;
63 Tim Street-Porter/Architect Brian Murphy;
64 Trevor Richards;
65 above right Bent Rej;
65 above left Bent Rej;
65 below The Interior World/Fritz von der Schulenburg (Lesley Howell);
72 above left Elizabeth Whiting & Associates/Tim Street-Porter;
72 below Paul Ryan/International Interiors/designer Lahtinen;
73 above Elizabeth Whiting & Associates/Tom Leighton/Architect Jan Kaplicky;
73 below Arcaid/Richard Bryant/Architect Jan Kaplicky;
74 Marie Claire Maison/Marie-Pierre Morel/Julie Borgeaud;
74-75 Paul Ryan International

Interiors/designer James Gager;
82 The Interior World/Fritz von der Schulenburg (Andrew Wadsworth);
83 The Interior World/Fritz von der Schulenburg/ designer Jacques Grange;
84 Arcaid/Richard Bryant/Architect John Young;
85 Tim Street-Porter/Architect Frank Israel
86 The Interior World/Fritz von der Schulenburg (Andrew Wadsworth);
87 Paul Ryan/International Interiors/designer House & House;
94 Marie Claire Maison/Gilles de Chabaneix/Catherine Ardouin;
94-95 Marie Claire Maison/Jacques Primois/Postic;
102 Elizabeth Whiting & Associates/Andreas von Einsiedel;
102-103 Elizabeth Whiting & Associates/Jerry Harpur;
104 Robert Harding Picture Library/JHC Wilson;
104-105 Bent Rej;

Special photography by Michael Crockett: 1, 5, 8, 10 below, 11 above, 12 above, 13 right, 14-15, 18-19, 21-27, 29 below, 32-37, 44-49, 56-61, 66-71, 76-81, 88-93, 96-101, 106-133.